GUIDE TO THE HOLY LAND

THEODERICH
GUIDE TO THE HOLY LAND

TRANSLATED BY
AUBREY STEWART

*

SECOND EDITION
WITH NEW INTRODUCTION,
NOTES AND BIBLIOGRAPHY
BY
RONALD G. MUSTO

ITALICA PRESS
NEW YORK
1986

First Published 1897
Committee of the Palestine Exploration Fund
Palestine Pilgrims' Text Society
London

*

Second Edition
Copyright © 1986 by Italica Press

ITALICA PRESS, INC.
625 Main Street
New York, New York 10044

Library of Congress Cataloging-in-Publication Data

Theodericus, of Würzburg, fl. 1172.
    Guide to the Holy Land

    Translation of: Libellus de locis sanctis.
    Bibliography: p.
    Includes index.
    1. Palestine--Description and travel. 2. Theodericus, of Würzburg, fl. 1172--
Journey--Palestine. 3. Christian pilgrims and pilgrimages--Palestine. I. Musto, Ronald
G. II. Title.
DS105.T4713 1986   915.694'4043   86-46119
ISBN 0-934977-03-8 (pbk.)

Printed in the United States of America
5 4 3 2 1

Cover Illustration: Jerusalem, from Hartmann Schedel, *Nuremberg Chronicle*,
Nuremberg: Anton Koberger, 1493.

TEMPLE OF THE LORD c. 1490

CONTENTS

LIST OF ILLUSTRATIONS

PREFACE

The following book is a modernized version of Aubrey
Stewart's 1897 edition of Theoderich's *Description of the
Holy Land,* a translation of the *Libellus de locis sanctis*
published in volume 5 of the Palestine Pilgrims' Text
Society series. The present edition follows Stewart's
faithfully with a few modifications and additions. These
include the modernization of certain Victorian usages in
the text, including archaisms like "beginneth," modern -
izaton of capitalization and spelling, and the reorgani -
zation of some of Stewart's large text blocks into smaller
paragraphs. There was, happily, need for very few of
these changes, and Stewart's text shares the PPTS virtue
of highly readable English translations created in an era
when English prose had reached classic form.

To aid the reader in following and referring to the text
this edition has retained the original chapter numbers and
order but has also split the text into three parts for easier
reference. These are:

I. The description of Jerusalem proper (1-18)
II. The description of the area around Jerusalem,
    including the Mount of Olives, Bethany, and
    Bethphage (19-27)
III. The rest of the Holy Land (28-51).

The annotations to this edition are intended to supplement Stewart's own with the findings of modern studies on the geography, topography, and archeology of the Holy Land and with appropriate historical informa - tion where necessary. Many of Stewart's original citations, shortened in the expectation that they would be comprehensible to the readers of the Palestine Pilgrims' Series, have been expanded to conform with modern methods or, where superceded by modern findings, replaced altogether. There is no intention to present any original research but to provide the reader with some of the best contemporary studies available. The biblio - graphy both offers a supplement to the sources noted by Stewart and provides a solid introduction to the area of study for anyone who might want to pursue a topic further.

The illustrations accompanying the text are drawn from high or late medieval sources and are included to show some of the sites in the Holy Land and the geographical world of the Mediterranean in the Middle Ages. The maps of Jerusalem and the Holy Land that accompany the text are original to this edition.

* *
*

PREFACE
TO
THE FIRST EDITION

Nothing certain seems to be known of Theoderich except his name.[1] It is probable that he is the Dietrich mentioned in John of Würzburg's "Introductory Epistle," but there is no certain proof of this, nor have we any means of identifying him with "Theodericus, Praepositus de Werdea," or "Theodericus, Praepositus de Onolsbach," whom we find mentioned in the records of Würzburg at the end of the twelfth century. Probably, as is stated in the Preface to John of Würzburg,[2] he was that Theoderich who became Bishop of Würzburg in 1223. He was, we know, a German and, almost certainly, a Rhinelander; for he tells us how on Palm Sunday he and his companions buried their fellow-pilgrim named Adolf of Cologne in the Potter's Field near Jerusalem, while the comparison of the Church of the Holy Sepulchre at Jerusalem with the church at Aix la Chapelle proves that he was familiar with that country.

Theoderich and John of Würzburg in many parts of their narratives, especially when describing what they did not personally behold, agree very closely, using in some instances the same words. They may have copied one another, but it seems more probable that both of them, or at any rate John of Würzburg, as also Eugesippus Fretillus and other writers, copied this part from a brief geographical and historical account of the Holy Land and its neighbourhood which was then much in men's hands, and which will here for the sake of shortness be called "the old compendium." A certain amount of light is given us by the expressed intention of John of Würzburg to write only about Jerusalem and its neighbourhood — "the holy places within and without the walls being those which alone we mean to describe...whereas we have no intention of giving any account of those which are in the neighbouring province, knowing that enough has been already said about them by other writers." It is worthy of remark that Thietmar[3] does the exact opposite of this, although there was much to be said about Jerusalem, because that city had already been thoroughly described by many writers. Indeed, John of Würzburg does not carry out his intention, since he gives a circumstantial account of the holy places of Galilee also, whereby he excites the suspicion that in so doing he merely acted as a copyist, since one would not willingly suppose that the account of the more distant regions was added to that of the topography of Jerusalem and its neighbourhood by another hand.

Theoderich starts with the distinct declaration that his description rests partly upon what he himself saw, and partly upon trustworthy accounts received from others;[4] but even when he is dealing with these "trustworthy accounts" or with the "old compendium," he proceeds far more self-reliantly than John. Moreover, his narrative, besides being fuller, contains many vivid touches which are wanting in the other. The people shouting their "Dex aide" and "Holy Sepulchre" while awaiting the descent of the holy fire on Easter Day "not without tears;" the stacking up of the pilgrims' crosses on the top of the rock of Calvary, and the bonfire made of them on Easter Eve;

the ignorant pilgrims who piled up heaps of stones in the valley of Hinnom and expected to sit upon them in the Day of Judgment; the account of how terribly he and his companions were alarmed at the Saracens — "un peuple criard," Kinglake calls the Arabs in "Eothen," quoting Lamartine — who were beginning to plough up a field by the side of the road to Shechem, and yelling horribly, "as is their wont when they are setting about any piece of work;" the description of what he saw with his own eyes (*vidimus*) of the wealth and charity of the Hospitallers, and of the power of the Templars; the Norman-French names of "Belmont," "Fontenoid," and "Montjoye," which sound so strangely in the country of the Bible; the throng of ships in the dangerous harbour of Acre, with his own "buss" amongst them; and the view from the Mountain of Temptation over the wide darkling plain, covered with numberless pilgrims, each bearing a torch, and watched, no doubt, by the "infidels" on the Arabian hills beyond Jordan — all these are invaluable helps towards forming a picture of the Holy Land in the time of the Frankish kings.

A distinction must be made between what Theoderich saw and what he only describes by hearsay; the former is clear, complete, and full of new facts, while the latter is brief, and, as a rule, confusedly written. He appears to have landed at Acre (Ptolemais), journeyed thence to Jerusalem, visited Jericho and the Jordan, and returned by the same road, although he may have personally visited Nazareth by way of Tiberias and Mount Tabor. His account of the Sea of Gennesareth is hopelessly confused, probably through copyists' errors. However, he not only describes clearly all that he saw, but describes it so naively and intelligently as to win the reader's esteem.

Our Saviour lies nearer his heart than anyone else. He speaks of His Mother with due respect, but shows no trace of the mariolatry of later ages. He is superior to many travellers of the present day in that he directs no sarcasm against men of other faiths;[5] and one can hardly expect to find in him the modern historical and critical spirit. The book contains so few of the pious reflections behind which men often conceal their ignorance of the affairs of this life, that one could wish for more and fuller expressions of the writer's personal feelings. Such as there are are upright and honourable, and are spoken from the heart. Although the writer, as we learn from Chapter XXIX, was a priest, he never obtrudes his priestly dignity upon us; indeed, it seems almost strange that he never alludes to having read prayers, or even having performed his devotions at any of the holy places. At the period at which he wrote, spiritual things were held in honour as a matter of course, so that it appeared unnecessary for him to make any effort to excite the feelings of his readers or hearers.

There can be no doubt that the pilgrimage of Theoderich took place in the time of the Crusaders, before their expulsion from Jerusalem in 1187. A number of particulars prove that he sojourned in the city while it was still under the rule of the Frankish kings. All we have left to do is to fix the exact year. In Chapter XXX, we read that Emaded-Din Zenghi, called Sanginus or Sanguineus,[6] beheaded six monks in a monastery on the banks of the Jordan. This apparently took place in 1138, when the Turks crossed the Jordan, and made a plundering raid through the districts of Jericho and Tekoa. Eight years after this "razzia" Zenghi was murdered. In Chapter XII we find the name of the patriarch Fulcher, who held the patriarchate from 1146 to 1157.

In the Temple of the Lord, Theoderich,[7] besides the date 1101, read that it was finished in the sixty-third year after the taking of Jerusalem, which brings us to the year 1164. In Chapter XLV we find it mentioned that Paneas was taken by the Mohammedans in the year 1171. The description of the tombs of the kings in Chapter XII brings us down to Amaury or Amalrich, who died on the 11th of June, 1173.

Thus it appears that 1173 is the latest date mentioned: the next thing to be considered is whether the tombs were rightly pointed out to him, which is no very easy matter. Theoderich came from the Chapel of St. Helena into the great Church of the Holy Sepulchre, and proceeded into the south transept, with the altar close by to the southward. Here he mentions five[8] tombs on the south side in front of the door, whereof the first, being that of the brother of the reigning King of Jerusalem (Baldwin III), was abutting on the choir of the canons, which is called at the present day the *Catholicon* of the Greek Church. In case the words "the tomb of the brother of the King of Jerusalem, named Baldwin," should not be sufficiently clear, the explanation, I think, is given by the sentence: "The fourth tomb is that of the father of the present king, that is, of Amalrich." According to chronological order the tombs are as follows:

First Godfrey's, which stands third as you go from the tomb of Baldwin III towards the choir, next to Baldwin II's.

Secondly, Baldwin I's, the second in the row.

Thirdly, that of Baldwin II (du Bourg), the father of Queen Milicent, and of Judith, the Abbess of St. Lazarus of Bethany, the fifth in the row.

Fourthly, Fulke's, the father of Baldwin III, and of Amalrich, the fourth in the row.

And fifthly, that of Baldwin III, the first in the row.

Now, no one can deny that Theoderich made his pilgrimage to the Holy Land during the life-time of King Amalrich, who reigned from 1162 to 1173. It is very important to observe that the tomb of Baldwin III was pointed out as that of the brother of the king, because the actually reigning king was assumed to be well known, and, therefore, one easily sees why his tomb does not occur in the list, because he was still alive. We have already, therefore, mention of the year 1171, and we must not go beyond the year 1173, in which Amalrich died, so that the pilgrimage of Theoderich must have taken place between the year 1171 and 1173.

Other less definite considerations point to the same date. Theoderich says of the Chapel of the Holy Sepulchre,[9] that on account of the partial fading of the colours he was quite unable to read the inscriptions on the arches; which is a proof that he made his visitation late, yet not at the very latest time, since we do not hear of the chapel being divided into two parts,[10] and Phocas dwells especially upon the fact that the Emperor Manuel Comnenus, who reigned from 1143 to 1180, entirely covered the sepulchre with gilding. It is very likely that Theoderich saw the Chapel of the Sepulchre during the time of its restoration, since, although he could not read the faded inscriptions, he tells us that he read the antiphonal hymn *Christus resurgens* in golden letters, whereas John of Würzburg describes it as in silver letters. Theoderich saw the gilded turret above the chapel with its dome and cross when the gilding was bright and fresh, John merely speaks of a cupola covered with silver; which proves, what we have already gathered from the "Introductory Epistle" of the latter, that he was the precursor of Theoderich.[11] From Theoderich we also learn that the Templars were engaged in building a new church on Mount Moriah, about which he uses the same expression as John of Würzburg, who says: "*Cum extructione novae ecclesiae nondum tamen consum - matae.*"[12] Moreover, the theory that John was the earlier pilgrim is supported by the latter's remark that at Shechem "a church is now being built" over Jacob's Well, whereas Theoderich speaks of it as being already built. It does not, however, seem to accord with this evidence that Theoderich speaks of the church of the Pater Noster, or of our Saviour, as "being now building," whereas John speaks of it as already built. At any rate, we may gather from this that the two pilgrimages left but a short interval between them. Lastly, we may remark that Theoderich mentions a new cistern on the way from Jerusalem to Bethlehem, in his description of the valley of Hinnom, which, without doubt, was the Lacus Germani, the *Birket es-Sultan* of the present day, of which we find no other mention previous to 1176. On the other hand, we know that the well of Job (Bir Eyûb), at the confluence of Hinnom and Cedron, was first discovered by Germanus in 1184, and could not, therefore, be alluded to by Theoderich.

From internal evidence we learn that Theoderich's pilgrimage took place in the spring of the year, at the *passagium vernale*, in March, or Easter, not the *passagium aestivale*, in August, on St. John's Day. Theoderich saw ripe barely in the plain of Jericho on the Monday after Palm Sunday, and on the Wednesday in Easter week he was at Acre on his way home.

The references in the notes are to the English translations of the pilgrims.[13]

-Aubrey Stewart

NOTES

1. Stewart relies for his preface on that of Tobler's Latin edition.

2. John of Würzburg, *Description of the Holy Land*, Aubrey Stewart, trans., London: Palestine Pilgrims' Text Society, 1896; reprint ed., New York: AMS, 1971, pp. ix-x.

3. See *Die Chronik des Thietmar von Merseburg*, trans. M. Laurent in *Geschichtschreiber der deutschen Vorzeit*, 2: xxvi, Leipzig, 1892.

4. Prologue, chaps. 25 and 51, pp. 1, 41 and 73.

5. With the exception of the Jews, against whom he levels many of the charges common in the anti-Semitic literature of the day. See Introduction, p. xxiii.

6. See Edward Gibbon, *The History of the Decline and Fall of the Roman Empire*, London: Methuen, 1912; reprint ed., New York: AMS, 1974, chap. 59.

7. Chap. 15, p.26.

8. Stewart provides an appendix closely examining the historical evidence for the tombs and the list of Latin kings that follows below. This appendix has been omitted in the present edition.

9. See chap. 5, p. 10.

10. See John Phocas, *The Pilgrimage of Johannes Phocas*, London: Palestine Pilgrims' Text Society, 1896; reprint ed., New York: AMS, 1971, p. 19; and Innominatus, IV, in *Anonymous Pilgrims*,

trans. Aubery Stewart, London: Palestine Pilgrims' Text Society, 1894; reprint ed., New York: AMS, 1971, chap. 15.

11. See chap. 5, p. 10 and n. 25.

12. Although the construction of the new church was yot yet completed.

13. This is a reference to the publications of the Palestine Pilgrims' Text Society (Committee of the Palestine Exploration Fund), which published annotated English translations of the medieval guides to the Holy Land during the last decade of the 19th century. Stewart's translation of Theoderich, as well as several other works translated and edited by him, appeared in this series.

* *
*

THEODERICH'S WORLD
Sallust-Type Map c. 1200

Based on ancient and medieval "T-O" types, this map divides
the circle of the world into three parts. The map is "oriented,"
that is, East appears at the top, above the largest division of
Asia. Europe is at the left, and Africa at the right. The
continents are divided by the "T" of oceans. The arms are the
Hellespont and Nile, the stem the Mediterranean. At the center,
where the continents and seas meet, is the Holy Land, with
Jerusalem, the large three-towered city with crosses, at the
center of the world. Tyre and Sidon are below the squiggle of
"Libanus" to the left of the city. Rome is the four-towered city
in the left division; the Alps are the three peaks to its left
(north). The Rhine flows at the bottom left.

INTRODUCTION

Theoderich's *Guide to the Holy Land* is one of the best known and most widely used of the medieval pilgrims' guides to Jerusalem and the Holy Land. Written around 1172 by the German monk Theoderich, it is a complete guide to the city's sacred sites and history, as well as to the legends and places of historical interest in the medieval Crusader State as they were only fifteen years before the destruction of the kingdom by Saladin.

Since the first publication of Aubrey Stewart's edition of *Theoderich's Description of the Holy Places* in 1897, scholars have made great strides in understanding the world that Theoderich described. The fields of Crusade history, especially the discussion of the institutions, economy, social life and customs of the Latin Kingdom, of travel literature and the history of trade and navigation in the Middle Ages, and the study of popular spirituality — most especially of the cult of the saints and of pilgrimage — and the related movements of the Twelfth Century Renaissance have all shed significant light on the era of the Crusades. This introduction is intended to survey some of these findings and to highlight some of the elements of Theoderich's *Guide* not covered by Stewart's preface that would be of interest to a modern reader.

THEODERICH

Little more is known about Theoderich's life and work than what Stewart offered, except for the suggestion that he was a monk of Hirsau, the autonomous abbey about 40 miles east of Strasbourg. Most recently this theory has been summarized by François Dolbeau[1] and rests on internal evidence and on the new paleographical inter - pretation of an abbreviation of Theoderich's place of origin in the Latin text of his guide,[2] from *Herbipolensis,* or "of Würzburg" to *Hirsaugiensis,* or "of Hirsau." The fact that the only other manuscript of the work, now in Minneapolis,[3] derives from the monastery of St. Barbara in Cologne also points to the Rhine Valley origin of the work and its author.

From Theoderich's detailed descriptions of the archi - tecture of the Holy Land, especially the Church of the Holy Sepulcher in Jerusalem, his notation of columns and piers, of drums and domes, of stairways, windows and arches, from his comments on the uses and juxtaposition of these elements, from his apparent knowledge of build - ing materials, of marbles and stone, of housing styles, and his accurate comparison to buildings in Europe, one could also gather that he was familiar with at least the vocabulary of architecture, and may himself have been an architect.

At the same time we should note his almost complete distinterest in the political situation in the Latin Kingdom or in its neighbors. For someone so observant of materi - als and styles, this complete disregard for personalities and policies offers an interesting insight into the psycho - logical world of a medieval pilgrim. For Theoderich, and his readers, it was the sacred geography of the pilgrim, not the political geography of the crusader, that really mattered.

In another area Theoderich also seems to have been a man of his time: the anti-Semitism that, if certainly not universal, was at least widespread both in his native Rhineland and in the Latin Kingdom during the Crusade period.[4] His repetition of several incidents in the New Testament in which the Jews are reported to have sought to harm Jesus or were actually blamed for his crucifixion are supplemented here by other tales. These include the story of the Jew who attempted to steal the Virgin Mary's veil from her tomb in chapter 23 (pp. 38-39) and the story in chapter 50 (p. 71) of the Jews of Beirut who attempted to repeat the torments of Christ on his image. While much of Theoderich's prejudice may have traveled with his pilgrim's baggage, he may also have picked up these stories from his Latin guides at the sites he describes or from the written sources he used to supplement his own account.

THE TWELFTH-CENTURY RENAISSANCE

We should also understand Theoderich's guide in the context of the cultural and intellectual movements of his age. Chief among these is the Twelfth Century Renais-sance,[5] the general revival of interest in ancient learning and piety that extended to all aspects of religious and intellectual life. This Renaissance saw proper models for the present age in the imitation of the pure sources of antiquity, whether Christian or pagan. Thus the century witnessed the revival of Aristotle for the methods and subjects of philosophical discussion, as well as the absorption of Greek science and geography, of Roman law and grammatical tracts, a revival of Latin poetry and history writing, and a renewed interest in the classics of Christian learning: the Greek and Latin Fathers of the early church.

In religious life this Renaissance meant a great evangelical awakening, as itinerant preachers and new religious orders attempted to revive the spiritual life of Christendom through the literal imitation of the poverty, humility, and charity of the Gospels and of the early church. Thus groups like the Waldensians and the Franciscans at the end of the century and reformers as diverse as Arnold of Brescia and Bernard of Clairvaux set about to live the evangelical life of simple imitation. At the same time a series of "second" popes, such as Innocent II, Urban II and Anacletus II, took names that recalled the very first Roman popes of the early church and so pointed to these figures of Christian antiquity as concrete models of Christian leadership.

While the historical consciousness of the time certainly saw nothing like the critical approach of modern history writing and archeological study, the twelfth century did witness a new critical attitude to the study of the Bible.[6] The study of the sacred texts became the model for all forms of learning from the liberal arts to historical narrative and theological speculation; while the events of the New Testament and the sacred history and places of the Old Testament were studied with renewed interest for both scriptural exegesis and factual information and were well known to all educated people.

POPULAR SPIRITUALITY

This renewed interest in Christian antiquity coincided with, and no doubt reflected, the same impulses as the new popular spirituality of the time.[7] As never before in Christian history the people of the West now began to turn to Gospel imitation in larger and larger numbers. Two of the best known examples of this spirit were, paradoxically, the renewed interest in the cult of the saints and the related rise in the number and extent of pilgrimages to their shrines.

Believing that the relics of the saints and the centers of their cults possessed great spiritual and historical power that enabled the faithful to participate in the saint's closeness to God, medieval men and women began flocking to the shrines of the most renowned in record numbers. Thus pilgrimages to such venerated sites as St. James of Compostela in northern Spain, to the sites of the martyrdoms of Peter and Paul in Rome, and to the most sacred sites of Jerusalem and the Holy Land gave the pilgrim the ability to literally relive the life and suffer-ings of the saints and so repeat the sacred and heroic deeds of antiquity in the present time.[8] The pilgrimage journey itself and the hardships that it involved also allowed pilgrims to expiate their own guilt for sins. The further off the pilgrimage site and the more difficult the journey, the better the imitation.

Thus the journey to Jerusalem held out the greatest prospect for grace as both the most difficult, perilous, and remote of pilgrimage sites; while the ability to literally and physically retrace the footsteps of Christ and the apostles consummated the meaning of religious reform in the twelfth century. In Jerusalem and the other sacred places of the Holy Land the pilgrim could reexperience the sufferings of their Savior and gain the benefits of his death in grace and forgiveness.

In addition to this act of penitence and grace, the journey to Jerusalem also held deep mystical and legend-ary meaning for medieval men and women, for the sacred city was believed to be the center of the world, the *omphalos* or navel, the sacred hub of the world's orb.[9] At the same time, it was the ideal of the sacred city — for Jerusalem was both the center of Christian history, the stage of Christ's redemptive sacrifice and resurrection, and the end of all history. It was, as the book of the *Apocalypse* assured its readers, the city of the final days, the heavenly city that would be granted by heaven to replace the kingdom of the world, whether of Rome or of Babylon.

Medieval people fully understood that this Heavenly Jerusalem[10] was a mystical goal that ended and tran-scended history. It was the last and best city, whose walls were jaspar, whose foundations were fixed with precious jewels, whose twelve gates were pearls, and whose streets were paved with gold. Yet for many the heavenly city, the goal of history, was confused with the earthly city, the center of the physical globe and the goal of earthly pilgrimage. Thought of the earthly Jerusalem could, and often did, strike deep chords of mystical and apocalyptic expectation, while with the eleventh and twelfth centuries many saw their pilgrimages to the city, whether armed or unarmed, as a fulfillment of the prophesies in the *Apocalypse* and hoped that reaching the physical city would bring the bliss of the elect promised by the vision of the *heavenly* city.[11]

THE ROUTE TO JERUSALEM

Pilgrimage may have been an act of apocalyptic spirituality, penitence for sin, and of evangelical imitation; yet it was also the opportunity to travel and to explore, whether this meant a week's excursion to a local shrine or the ultimate pilgrimage, the journey to *Outremer,* the land across the sea. As such the pilgrimage offers us many valuable and fascinating glimpses into the material life of the Middle Ages: of geographical knowledge and lore, and of medieval travel, its seasons, conditions, duration, forms of transport, food, booking arrangements, contracts and costs, dangers and pleasures.

By the late twelfth century, of course, the path of the pilgrim, well trodden since at least the fourth century, had been deepened and widened by the Crusades.[12] Launched in 1095, the First Crusade had conquered Jerusalem and surrounding Palestine as far south as Gaza and the Sinai and as far north as Tripoli in Lebanon and east as far as Edessa (Urfa) in modern Turkey. The expedition had followed well known pilgrimage routes. The land routes lead from southeastern Germany: Regensburg along the Danube and through the Balkans to Constantinople. Here it met the southern, Italian, route across the Adriatic from Brindisi or Bari to Dyrrhachium in modern Albania, which from there followed the ancient Via Egnatia across the Balkans to the Byzantine capital. The land route then led the pilgrim and crusader through Asia Minor: Nicea, south to Iconium, then along the coast via Tarsus or through the interior through Caesarea until the roads converged at the Cilician Gates and poured out into Syria at Antioch. At that point the land route left the Byzantine Empire for the Crusader states.

The pilgrim's other alternative was the sea route, no less dangerous due to the constant threat of piracy, but perhaps quicker in the proper season and at least unhindered by tolls, greedy princes or hostile tribes along the way. Many pilgrims thus made their way to the great Mediterranean ports: Genoa and Pisa or, if coming from central Europe, across the Alps to Venice. Marseille served intermittently for French pilgrims and Crusaders. From these shipping centers, bustling and prosperous city-states in the twelfth century, the pilgrim's company would sign up with a shipping company that dealt almost exclusively in the pilgrimage trade, carrying the faithful in large tours eastward and returning home from the Levant with high-profit cargos of spices, jewels, silks, ivory, sugar — and slaves — supplemented by returning pilgrims, lightened of at least their European sins and most of their travel funds.

Once in an Italian port[13] Theoderich and his com - panions may have taken advantage of one of the many advertised specials offered by the pilgrim agencies: special fares, including accommodations and food on board, tours of the Holy Land, and return voyage. Accommodations there were provided by the many inns or pilgrim hospices. Most pilgrim sailings were set for the spring, the *passagium vernale,* some in the summer passage, the *passagium aestivale.* Most pilgrims then spent the spring or summer in Outremer and returned with the southerly wind no later than September or October. Few sailings were ever made in the winter, when the brutal north winds brought occasional snows and constant storms throughout the Mediterranean.

By the end of the Crusades, in the fourteenth century, pilgrim ships could carry as many as 1,000 passengers with crew and cargo. These ships included both huge galleys, lanteen rigged and equipped with oars, the favored form of Mediterranean transport into the nine - teenth century, or the more sturdy and roomy "buss," the great round ships with some square rig on which Theoderich sailed, some of which measured over 100 feet long, 40 feet wide and weighed up to 1,000 tons. The average ship was about half this size.

Accommodations were less than luxurious.[14] All but the most wealthy pilgrims would consider themselves lucky if the travel mat that they carried tied to their backpack or stowed in their travel chests was laid in the same spot every night and provided enough room to stretch out. Most days were spent above decks, meals had to be simple due to the constant danger of fire from open hearths on board. Yet meals were provided, and these usually consisted of the pilgrim bread, *biscotum,* supplemented by sweet wine, some cheese and scanty vegetables, salted meat and whatever provisions the wise pilgrim — like the traveler on the Istanbul Express today — managed to gather together before embarking.

Cleanliness aboard ships was minimal, sleeping quarters were infested with lice, vermin and rats, fresh foods and water went bad after only a few weeks if not replenished. Considering the fact that most of the pilgrim's cabin companions had just come from a month or two on foot across Europe, and that some had already taken ascetic vows not to bathe or to clean their hair, all in all the journey really must have been an act of imitation of the early martyrs. Yet it was a special type of martyrdom that the traveler has always willingly embraced, that had its own mortifications as well as its own spiritual rewards. Landlocked Europeans experienced the sun and warmth of Mediterranean lands and saw, smelt, and felt the high seas for the first time in their lives. Pilgrims from small villages and towns visited lands of legend and enchant - ment: Italy and perhaps Sicily, St. Paul's Malta, Morea and Achaia in Greece, Crete and Cyprus, not to mention the fabled cities of the Levant, and Jerusalem itself.

If all went well with wind, ship, and safety, usually in a ship convoy — the journey eastward could take as little as four weeks, with stops at coastal ports and islands all along the way, and as long as eight to ten weeks against contrary winds, or if layed up for repairs. Pilgrims traveling via Genoa and Pisa generally followed these cities' trade routes to Acre (Acco or Ptolomais), while Venetian ships made land at their *fondaco* or emporium in Tyre. Theoderich, then, probably made his journey up the Rhine valley to Bavaria and then crossed the Alps and Lombardy before reaching either Genoa or Pisa. We assume this since he tells us that he departed from Acre (chapter 40, p. 59), and his narrative seems to indicate that this is where he also began his itinerary.

At Acre, the pilgrim port closest to Jerusalem, the pious traveler would pass through customs clearance and then choose a route:[15] either via Galilee, bearing north toward Lake Tiberias (Sea of Galilee) and then south through Samaria and Judaea to Jerusalem, or the pilgrim could take the southern, more direct, Seaside Road to the city. This seems to have been the way Theoderich's com - pany passed, since the sites he describes in Part III roughly follow this itinerary: Acre, Mount Carmel, south down the coast passed Chateau Pelerin, Caesarea and Jaffa, Lydda, Ramleh, and from there inland through Beit

Nuba and the Judaean Hills. He also vividly describes the Jezreel Valley south and east of Mount Carmel, and so must have also crossed this region at some time during his stay. Finally, approaching Jerusalem from the north, Theoderich would have reached the crest of Montjoye, the pilgrim's first joyous sight of the sacred city spread out below.

By 1172 Jerusalem probably had a population of about 30,000 out of a total population for the kingdom of nearly 250,000. Acre led the list with about 60,000 people. Tyre boasted about 40,000. Though large by northern European standards, these numbers were small by Mediterranean, especially Middle Eastern, norms. There were also about 20 cities with populations of around 5,000 spread across the Latin Kingdom. The Latin popu - lation, which tended to concentrate in the cities, has been estimated at about 100,000.[16]

In Part I Theoderich lays out all the standard sights in Jerusalem in excellent order and vivid description. He seems to have followed the western route through the city, the path that placed the Via Dolorosa, or the route of Christ's passion and death, from Mount Sion on the south, northeast to the Antonia fortress, and then west to Mount Calvary and the Holy Sepulcher.

Immediately outside the city Theoderich also followed the standard tour to Bethany and Bethphage to the east of the Kedron Valley and Mount of Olives. From there he seems to have joined one of the tours heading out to the Jordan Valley, including Mount Quarantana, the Jordan itself, and the reputed site of Christ's baptism. After stopping at the oasis of Jericho, he then probably returned via Jerusalem before heading to Bethlehem and Hebron in the Judaean Hills to the south.

His knowledge of regions further south and east — the Dead Sea, Transjordan, and Arabia — is mostly second-hand, a combination of hearsay, legend, and other accounts. But Theoderich does seem to have traveled to the southwest, to Gaza and Ascalon, standard stops on a pilgrim's tour. Returning again to Jerusalem, Theoderich then made a series of day or week trips, much like the modern tourist: to Emmaus, Ramatha, Shiloh, certainly north to Nablus (Neapolis), and Nazareth, and may even have traveled as far north as Tiberias on the Sea of Galilee.

It seems almost certain that he could not have traveled further north than that, since he describes the city of Banyas as being in Christian hands, when it was actually taken by Nur ed-Din a decade before. His descriptions of the sources of the Jordan in the underground river of Dan and the Jor probably confuses actual descriptions of marshes north of Lake Hulah with medieval legends about these two streams. His descriptions of most of Galilee, Idumea, Syria, Phoenicia, including Beirut and modern Lebanon, depend on biblical passages and legend.

Theoderich almost certainly visited Tyre, perhaps on his way back to the coast, and gives a vivid, if succinct, description of the city, its walls, double harbor, and great harbor chain. From there he seems to have traveled south along the coast back to Acre, from which he departed.[17]

GEOGRAPHICAL KNOWLEDGE

Many of the sites Theoderich describes in the Holy Land and specifically in Jerusalem are so accurately drawn that he has become a major source for medieval knowledge of the region, Jerusalem's topography, and the history of the art and archeology of the kingdom.[18] His work still offers valuable descriptions of fields full of ripe barley or roses, groves of palm or olive, orchards, various stone and soil types, of Moslems living in the Crusader state carrying on their customary agricultural routine with their own work routines and songs.

Much of his description of the border lands of the Holy Land, however, are rather fanciful. We have already mentioned places, such as the sources of the Jordan, for which he relies on second-hand sources like the "old compendium," and regions where he could not have been both because the topography he describes is incorrect and the political situation out of date. Yet even here his *Guide* is a valuable resource for the light it sheds on the geographical lore of the Middle Ages and on the age's sacred geography. Here we find Jerusalem as center of the world, a cosmological fact marked clearly in its stones and pavements; here too are rivers that run underground, the Dead Sea that once a year, on the anniversary of the destruction of Sodom and Gomorra, throws up their stone and wood, and the pillar of salt that was once Lot's wife.

THE *GUIDE* AS TRAVEL LITERATURE

All in all, then, Theoderich's *Guide to the Holy Land* is an important monument in the history of travel literature, both in unique qualities of description and travel narrative and in its qualities common to the genre of pilgrims' guides.

The work derives from a long tradition of Christian geographies and itineraries carried over from ancient sources and supplemented by the Bible. Examples include the guides to the Holy Land[19] by the Bordeaux Pilgrim in 333, St. Silvia's voyage in 385, St. Jerome's description of St. Paula's journey in the fifth century, Antoninus Martyr and Theodosius in the sixth century, Arculfus in the seventh, and Bernard the Wise c. 870.

Pilgrim guides at the time of the Crusades[20] seem to have begun with that of Saewulf in 1102/3. Nearly contemporary with Theoderich are those of John of Würzburg, Rabbi Benjamin of Tudela, the Russian Abbot Daniel, and John Phocas, all referred to by Stewart in the preface and notes. Even by the early twelfth century, however, these guides had become standardized, often copied from two collections known as the "old" and "new compendium." While Theoderich does sometimes bor-row from these, as in his descriptions of the Desert Elim and Sinai in chapter 31, he is one of the unique guides of the period, for his account depends almost entirely on his own observation. Where it does not, he usually informs the reader that he had relied on secondary sources.

One must really wait until the mid-thirteenth century to find works of similar importance and first-hand immediacy: the narratives of mission journeys to central Asia and China[21] by the Franciscans John of Plano Carpini and Benedict the Pole (1245-27), William of Rubruck (1253-54) and John of Monte Corvino (1289-91), and the most famous medieval travel book, the *Travels* of Marco Polo (1269-92). By the fourteenth century the obvious fabrications of Sir John Mandeville's travels to the Orient reflect the closing of the Levant to Europeans once again as the Crusade movement ground to a halt and word of foreign lands came only from the occasional pens of missionaries in the east, or not at all.

— Ronald G. Musto

NOTES

1. "Théodericus, De locis sanctis. Un second manuscrit, provenant de Saint-Barbe de Cologne," *Analecta Bollandiana* 103, 1-2 (1985): 113-14. For recent acceptance of the theory see Harry W. Hazard, ed., *The Art and Architecture of the Crusader States*. Vol. 4 in *A History of the Crusades*, Kenneth M. Setton, ed., 6 vols., Madison, WI: University of Wisconsin Press, 1977, p. 412. On Hirsau see Pierre-Roger Gaussin, *Les Cohortes du Christ*, Rennes: Ouest France, 1985, pp. 120-21.

2. In the edition of M.L. and W. Bulst, *Theodericus, Libellus de locis sanctis*, Heidelberg: Editiones Heidelbergensis, 1976, p. 4. Like that of T. Tobler, *Theoderici libellus de locis sanctis*, St. Gall and Paris, 1865, this new edition is based on the only manuscript then known, Vienna, Österreichische Nationalbibliothek MS 3529, folios 192-207, dating from the fifteenth century. The most recent edition of the work is that of Sabino de Sandoli, O.F.M., *Itinera hierosolymitana crucesignatorum (saec. xii-xiii)*, vol. 2, Jerusalem: Franciscan Printing Press, 1980, which reproduces Tobler's Latin text along with a new Italian translation.

3. University Library, MS 13 +.1, folios 89-119. Discovered by Dolbeau.

4. See Steven Runciman, *A History of the Crusades*. 3 vols, New York: Harper & Row, 1964, 1: 134-41, 2: 295-96; Joshua Prawer, *The Crusaders' Kingdom*, New York: Praeger, 1972, pp. 57-59, 234-56; F.E. Peters, *Jerusalem*, Princeton, NJ: Princeton University Press, 1985, pp. 288-90, 327-29.

5. Among the best introductions are Charles Homer Haskins, *The Renaissance of the Twelfth Century*, Cleveland and New York:

Meridien, 1966; and Christopher Brooke, *The Twelfth Century Renaissance,* New York: Harcourt Brace Jovanovich, 1976.

6. See Beryl Smalley, *The Study of the Bible in the Middle Ages,* Notre Dame, IN: University of Notre Dame Press, 1970.

7. For a brief introduction see Rosalind and Christopher Brooke, *Popular Religion in the Middle Ages: Western Europe 1000-1300,* London: Thames & Hudson, 1984, especially pp. 14-30.

8. See the works of Labarge, Prescott, and Sumption in the bibliography.

9. See John Kirtland Wright, *The Geographical Lore in the Time of the Crusades,* New York: Dover, 1965, pp. 259-60; Mircea Eliade, *The Sacred and The Profane,* New York: Harper and Row, 1961, pp. 42-45 and 60-61.

10. The reference is from Apoc. 21:9-21.

11. Apoc. 21:22-27, 22:1-5. See, but treat cautiously, Norman Cohn, *The Pursuit of the Millennium,* New York: Harper & Row, 1961, pp. 40-52. Cohn tends to view all medieval millennial movements as expressions of popular, revolutionary, and violent tendencies.

12. For a description of the routes see Runciman, 1: 121-94.

13. On shipping in the Mediterranean see Fernand Braudel, *The Mediterranean and the Mediterranean World in the Age of Philip II,* 2 vols., New York: Harper & Row, 1972, 1: 103-67, 246-67; Robert S. Lopez and Irving W. Raymond, eds., *Medieval Trade in the Mediterranean World,* New York: W.W. Norton, 1967, pp. 239-337. For pilgrims' shipping, accommodations, voyages, etc. see Prawer, pp. 195-204; Hazard, pp. 44-47.

14. See Prawer, pp. 201-3; Hazard, pp. 46-50.

15. On routes see Prawer, pp. 204-13; Hazard, pp. 50-68.

16. See Hans Eberhard Mayer, *The Crusades,* New York: Oxford University Press, 1972, pp. 153-54; Prawer, pp. 82-83.

17. Stewart notes that Theoderich departed on Wednesday of Easter Week. But whether of the same year is doubtful; the sights visited certainly cover a wide range and reflect prolonged stay and

description. Such a journey to the Holy Land and back in one spring season seems highly improbable.

18. See for example Hazard, pp. 10-11, 117-18; Peters, pp. 321-22, 326-27.

19. For these and other guides see the volumes in the Palestine Pilgrims' Text Society, 1-3.

20. See Wright, pp. 115-18.

21. See Christopher Dawson, ed., *Mission to Asia*, New York: Harper & Row, 1966; *The Travels of Sir John Mandeville*, New York: Dover, 1964; and Marco Polo, *The Travels*, New York: Penguin Books, 1967.

* *
*

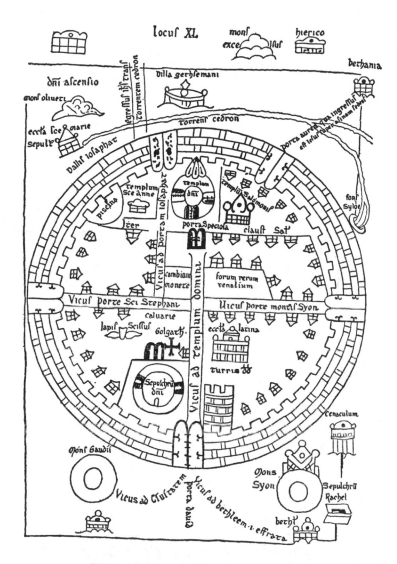

JERUSALEM c. 1200

The Holy City is shown as a circle, the ideal form. The map is "oriented," the East is at the top. Above the walls are the Valley of Josaphat and the Cedron Brook. Within the walls the circle is divided into four by the crossing of the Temple Street (bottom to top) and of St. Stephen's and Mount Sion Streets (left to right). The Temple of the Lord is the circle at the top; the Holy Sepulcher that in the bottom left. Outside the walls below are the circles of Mons Gaudii on the left and Mount Sion on the right. Other landmarks include the Temple of Solomon (top right), St. Anne's (top left), the Covered Market (center, right), and the Tower of David (bottom, center). Compare map on page 95.

PROLOGUE

THEODERICH, THE MEANEST OF ALL MONKS
and Christian men, addresses himself to all worshipers of
the holy and indivisible Trinity, and more especially to
the lovers of our most gracious Lord Jesus Christ.

So may they learn on earth below to share our Savior's pain,
That they with joy hereafter may deserve with him to reign.

We have been careful to note down, in writing on
paper, everything relating to the holy places where our
healer and Savior, when actually present in the flesh,
accomplished the duties and mysteries connected with his
blessed humanity and our salvation, which we have either
ourselves seen with our own eyes or have learned from
the truthful tales of others. This we have done in order
that, according to the best of our ability, we may satisfy
the desires of those who are unable to proceed there in
person by describing those things that they cannot see
with their own eyes or hear with their ears. Be it known
to our readers that we have labored at this task to the
intent that by reading this description or tale they may
learn always to bear Christ in remembrance, and by re -
membering him may learn to love him, by loving may
pity him who suffered near these places; through pity,
may acquire a longing for him, by longing for him may
be absolved from their sins; by absolution from sin may
obtain his grace, and by his grace may be made partakers
of the kingdom of heaven, being thought worthy of it by

1

him who with the Father and the Holy Spirit lives and reigns for ever and ever. Amen.

Here begins the little book written by Theoderich about the holy places.

* *
*

PART I

I

THE RUIN OF THE LAND
AND THE CHANGING OF ITS NAMES

It is evident to all who read the pages of the Old and New Testament that the land of Canaan was, by divine or - dinance, given as a possession to the twelve tribes of the people of Israel. This land, divided into the three pro - vinces of Judaea, Samaria, and Galilee, was in antiquity enriched by many cities, towns, and castles. The names and situations of all these cities were in former days well known to everyone; but the moderns, being strangers in the land, and not its original inhabitants, know only the names of a few places that we shall describe in their prop - er place. For since our dearest Lord Jesus Christ re - quired vengeance for his blood — which was shed on the cross by the cruel hands of the impious Jews — the Roman princes, Vespasian and Titus, entered Judaea with an army, leveled the Temple and city to the ground, de - stroyed all the cities and villages throughout Judaea, and drove the murderers themselves out of their own country and forced them to depart and live among foreigners. In consequence of this all works and constructions of that people, and of the entire province, have been destroyed, so that although some traces of certain places still remain, nearly all their names have been altered.

II

JUDAEA

First, then, we must speak of Judaea, which is known to have been the chief province of the Jewish kingdom, which we have been able to examine with our own eyes and ears. There, as an eye in the head, is placed the Holy City of Jerusalem, from which, through our mediator with God, our Lord Jesus Christ, grace and salvation and life have flowed to all nations. Judaea is bounded on the west by the Great Sea.[1] On the south it is separated by the desert from the mountains of Arabia and Egypt. On the east it is limited by the River Jordan, and on the north it is skirted by Samaria and Idumaea.[2]

Now Judaea is for the most part mountainous, and round about the Holy City rises into very lofty ranges, sloping on all sides down to its aforesaid boundaries, just as, on the other hand, one ascends to it from them. These mountains are in some places rough with masses of the hardest rock, in other places they are adorned with stone excellently suited to be cut into ashlar, and in others they are beautified by white, red, and variegated marble. But wherever any patches of earth are found among these masses of rock the land is seen to be fit for the production of every kind of fruit. We have seen the hills and moun - tains covered with such vineyards and plantations of olive trees and fig trees, and the valleys abounding with corn and garden produce.

III

JERUSALEM,
THE VALLEYS OF JOSAPHAT AND GEHINNOM,
MOUNT OF REJOICING *(MONS GAUDII)*,
TOMB OF JOSAPHAT,
POSITION OF THE HOLY CITY,
ITS FORTIFICATIONS, GATES, STREETS, HOUSES,
CISTERNS, WOOD

Now, on the very topmost peak of these mountains, as is
affirmed by both Josephus and Jerome, is placed the city
of Jerusalem, which is held to be holier and more notable
than all the other cities and places throughout the world,
not because it is holy in itself, or by itself, but because it
has been glorified by the presence of God himself, and of
our Lord Jesus Christ and his holy mother, and by the
dwelling there, the doctrine, the preaching, and the
martyrdom of patriarchs, prophets, Apostles, and other
holy people. Although it has mountain ridges higher than
itself all around it, it is itself hilly, being built on a moun -
tain. Hence it follows that it attracts the eyes of viewers
away from all the mountains by which it is surrounded.

Now, between the Hill of Moriah, on which stands the
Temple of the Lord, and the Mount of Olives, which
raises its head higher than any of the other mountains, lies
the Cedron Brook and the Valley of Josaphat. This valley
starts from the Mount of Rejoicing[3] *(Mons Gaudii)*, from
which one enters the city on the northern side, passes by
the Church of St. Mary, which is so called after her,
passes the Tomb of Josaphat,[4] king of Judaea, from whose
death it itself has received this name, and passes close to
the bathing Pool of Siloe, where another valley meets it.
This valley[5] bends its course from the right-hand corner
of the city past the new cisterns between Mount Sion and
the field of Acheldemach,[6] thus embracing two sides of
the city with a very deep ravine. The Tomb of Josaphat

stands in the midst of this valley, built of squared stone in the form of a pyramid. Round about it there are a great number of dwellings of servants of God, or hermits, all of which are placed under the care of the abbot of St. Mary's.[7]

Now, the longest part of the city reaches from north to south, and the width of it is from west to east, and it is most strongly fortified by walls and bastions on the top of the mountain above the aforesaid valleys. There is also a barrier, or fosse, placed outside the wall and furnished with battlements and loopholes, which they call the Barbican.[8] The city has seven gates, of which they firmly lock six every night until after sunrise; the seventh is closed by a wall and is only opened on Palm Sunday and on the day of the Exaltation of the Cross.[9]

Since it has an oblong form, the city has five angles, one of which is transverse. Almost all its streets are paved with great stones below, and above many of them are covered with a stone vault, pierced with many win- dows for the transmission of light. The houses,[10] which are lofty piles of carefully wrought stonework, are not finished with high-pitched roofs after our style but are level and flat. The people catch the rainwater that falls on them and store it up in cisterns for their own use — they use no other water, because they have none. Wood, suitable for building or for fires, is expensive there, because Mount Libanus — the only mountain that abounds in cedar, cypress, and pine wood — is a long way off from them, and they cannot approach it for fear of the attacks of the infidels.

IV

THE TOWER OF DAVID, MOUNTS SION AND MORIAH, THE FIELD OF ACELDAMA, MOUNT GION, THE HOUSE OF PILATE, ANTONIA

The Tower of David[11] is the property of the king of Jerusalem and is incomparably strong, being built of squared stones of immense size. It stands near the western gate, from which the road leads toward Bethlehem, together with the newly built solar chamber and palace that adjoins it, and it is strongly fortified with ditches and barbicans. It is situated on Mount Sion, of which we read in the Book of Kings (2 Sam. 5:7), "Now David took Sion." It is also situated over against the Temple of the Lord in the part of the city that extends sideways, with Mount Sion on the south and the Mount of Olives on the east. Mount Sion reaches from the tower as far as the Church of St. Mary outside the Walls[12] and from the church nearly as far as the Palace of Solomon and as far as the way that leads from the Beautiful Gate to the tower, being wider but lower than the Mount of Olives. Al - though Mount Moriah,[13] which overhangs the Valley of Josaphat and on which stands the Temple of the Lord and the Palace of Solomon, may be thought to be a great hill, Mount Sion surpasses it by as much as the latter seems to surpass the Valley of Josaphat.

In the Field of Acheldemach,[14] which is only separat - ed from it by the above-mentioned valley, is the pilgrims' burying ground, in which stands the Church of St. Mary, the Virgin Mother of God,[15] in which also on the holy day of Palm Sunday we buried one of our brethren, named Adolf, a native of Cologne. This field is overhung by Mount Gion, on which Solomon was crowned, as may be read in the Book of Kings.[16]

Of the other buildings, whether public or private, we have scarcely been able to find any traces, or at least very few, with the exception of the House of Pilate, near the Church of St. Anne, the mother of our Lady, which stands near the Sheep Pool.[17] Of all the work that Josephus tells us was built by Herod and is now utterly ruined, nothing remains save one side, which is still standing, of the palace that was called Antonia,[18] with a gate placed outside, near the court of the Temple.[19]

V

THE CHURCH OF THE HOLY SEPULCHER: THE CHAPEL

It only remains, then, that we should tell of the holy places, on account of which the city itself is called holy. We have thought, therefore, that it would be right to begin with the Holy of Holies; that is, with the sepulcher of our Lord.[20] The Church of the Holy Sepulcher, of marvelous skill, is known to have been founded by the Empress Helena. Its outer wall being carried, as it were, round the circumference of a circle, makes the church itself round. The place of our Lord's sepulcher occupies the central point in the church, and its form is that of a chapel built above the sepulcher itself and beautifully ornamented with a casing of marble. It is not in the form of a complete circle, but two low walls proceed from the circumference toward the east and meet a third wall. These walls contain three doors, three feet wide and seven feet high, one of which opens on the north, another on the east, and another on the south side. The entrance is by the northern door and the exit by the southern door. The eastern door is set apart for the use of the guardians of the sepulcher.[21]

Between these three small doors and the fourth door —
by which one goes into the sepulcher itself — is an altar
which, though small, is of great sanctity. On it our Lord's
body is said to have been laid by Joseph and Nicodemus
before it was placed in the sepulcher.[22] Above the actual
mouth of the sepulcher, which stands behind the altar,
these same men are shown in a picture of mosaic work[23]
placing our Lord's body in the tomb, with our Lady, his
mother, standing by, and the three Marys, whom we
know well from the Gospel, with pots of perfume, and
with the angel also sitting above the sepulcher and rolling
away the stone, saying, "Behold the place where they laid
him." (Mark 16:6.) Between the opening and the
sepulcher itself a line is drawn in a semicircular form,
which contains these verses:

> The place and guardian testify Christ's resurrection,
> Also the linen clothes, the angel, and Redemption.

All these things are portrayed in the most precious mosaic
work, with which the whole of this little chapel is
adorned.

Each of the doors has very strict porters, who will not
allow fewer than six, or more than twelve, people to enter
at one time; for, indeed, the place is so narrow that it will
not hold any more. After they have worshiped they are
obliged to go out by another door. No one can enter the
mouth of the sepulcher itself except by crawling upon
one's knees, and having crossed it, one finds that most-
wished-for treasure — I mean the sepulcher in which our
most gracious Lord Jesus Christ lay for three days —
which is wondrously adorned with white marble, gold
and precious stones.[24] In the side it has three holes,
through which the pilgrims give their long-wished-for
kisses to the very stone on which their Lord lay, which
measures two-and-one-half feet in width, and the length
of a man's arm from the elbow and one foot also. The

floor between the sepulcher itself and the wall is large enough to allow five people to pray on their knees with their heads turned toward the sepulcher.

Round about this building outside are arranged ten pillars, which, with the arches that they support, make a circular enclosure, beneath which is a base, having this text of Scripture carved on it in letters of gold:[25]

> Christ, having risen from the dead, dies no more.
> Death has no more dominion over Him
> For in that he lives,
> He lives in God. (Rom. 6:9-10.)

At his head, which was turned toward the west, there is an altar surrounded by partition walls, doors, and locks of iron, with lattice work of cypress wood decorated with various paintings, and with a roof of the same kind and similarly decorated, resting on the walls.[26] The roof of the work itself is formed of slabs of gilt copper, with a round opening in the middle, round which stand small pillars in a circle, carrying small arches above them, which support a cup-shaped roof. Above the roof itself is a gilded cross, and above the cross is a dove, likewise gilded.[27] Between every two columns throughout the circle, from each arch hangs a lamp. In the same manner two lamps hang between each of the lower columns all around the circle. Round the lower arches, on every arch, verses are written, some of which we were not able to read because of the fading of the colors. We were only able to read six plainly, which were written on three of the arches:

> Within this tomb was laid
> He who the world hath made:
> You who His tomb do see
> Haste you to be
> A temple meet for me.

Lamb of God blest!
Patriarchs old,
Longed, ere their rest,
Him to behold.

Brought forth at Ephrata,
Suffered at Golgotha.
He from his rocky bed,
Adam our father led,
    Bore him on high;
Conquered the devil's arts,
And said to sinking hearts,
    "Rise, it is I!"

Around the iron enclosure that, as we have said be -
fore, is placed at the head of the sepulcher, above which is
the lattice work, there runs a scroll containing these
verses:

'Twas here the victory o'er Death was won
And life for us begun;
To God the pleasing sacrifice was given,
The victim fell;
Our sins are all forgiven;
There is joy in heaven,
And grief in hell;
Ends the Old Testament,
God has a New one sent:
We learn from this, O Christ, who here has bled,
That holy is the ground whereon we tread.

VI

THE CHURCH OR ROTUNDA ITSELF

The pavement of this church is most beautifully laid with
Parian and various colored marble. The church itself is
supported below by eight square pillars, which are called
piers, and sixteen monolithic columns.[28] Above, since it
is vaulted both above and below like the church at Aix-la-

Chapelle, it is supported in the same fashion on eight piers and sixteen pillars. The lower string course, which runs around the whole church, is covered with inscriptions in Greek letters.

The surface of the wall that lies between the middle and the upper string courses glows with mosaic work of incomparable beauty. There, in front of the choir, that is, above the arch of the sanctuary, may be seen the boy Jesus wrought in the same mosaic,[29] but of ancient craft, depicted in glowing colors as far as the navel, with a most beautiful face; on his left hand his mother, and on his right the Archangel Gabriel pronouncing the well-known salutation, "Hail Mary, full of grace; the Lord is with thee, blessed among women, and blessed the fruit of thy womb." This salutation is written both in Latin and in Greek around the Lord Christ himself.

Further on, on the right side,[30] the twelve Apostles are depicted in a row in the same mosaic, each of them hold - ing in his hands praises of Christ in words alluding to the holy mysteries. In the midst of them, in a recess slightly sunken into the wall, sits in royal splendor, wearing the *trabea*,[31] the Emperor Constantine, because he, together with his mother Helena, was the founder of the church. Also beyond the Apostles, the blessed Michael the Archangel glitters in wondrous array. On the left follows a row of thirteen prophets, all of whom have their faces turned toward the beautiful boy, and reverently address him, holding in their hands the prophesies with which he inspired them of old. In the midst of them, opposite her son, sits the blessed Empress Helena, magnificently arrayed. On the wall itself rests a leaden roof supported by rafters of cypress wood, having a large round opening in the middle, through which the light comes from above and lights the whole church, for it has no other window at all.

VII

THE CHOIR OF THE CANONS

There adjoins this church a sanctuary,[32] or Holy of Holies, of marvelous skill, which was subsequently built by the Franks, who also most sweetly sing praises there[33] both by day and by night; that is to say, at the canonical hours, according to the cycle of the Virgin Mary. They hold prebends, and half the offerings of the Holy Sepul- cher is appropriated to them for income, while the other half is appropriated for the use of the patriarch. The high altar is dedicated to the name and in honor of our Lord and Savior, and behind it is placed the patriarch's seat, above which hang from the arch of the sanctuary a very great and adorable picture of our Lady, a picture of St. John the Baptist, and also a third picture of the holy Gabriel, her bridesman. In the ceiling[34] of the sanctuary itself is represented our Lord Jesus Christ holding his cross in his left hand, bearing Adam in his right, looking royally up toward heaven, with his left foot raised in a gigantic stride, his right still resting on the earth as he enters heaven,[35] while the following stand around — that is to say, his mother, St. John the Baptist, and all the Apostles. Under his feet a scroll, reaching across the arch from one wall to the other, contains this inscription:[36]

Praise Him crucified in the flesh,
Glorify Him buried for us,
Adore Him risen from death.

Beyond this, on a higher scroll drawn across the same arch, is the passage from Scripture, "Christ, ascending on high, he led away captives; he gave gifts to men." (Eph. 4:8.) About the middle of the choir there is a small open altar of great sanctity, on the flooring of which is marked a cross inscribed in a circle, which signifies that on this spot Joseph and Nicodemus laid our Lord's body in order to wash it after they had taken it down from the cross.[37] Before the door of the choir is an altar of no small size, which, however, is only used by the Syrians in their services. When the daily Latin services are over, the Syrians usually sing their hymns either there outside the choir, or in one of the apses of the church; indeed, they have several small altars in the church, arranged and devoted to their own peculiar use. These are the religious sects that celebrate divine service in the church at Jerusalem: the Latins, Syrians, Armenians, Greeks, Jacobites,[38] and Nubians.[39] All these differ from one another both in language and in their manner of conduct - ing divine service. The Jacobites use trumpets on their feast days, after the fashion of the Jews.

VIII

THE HOLY FIRE

It is customary in the Church of the Holy Sepulcher, both in the church itself and in all the other churches in the city, at daybreak on the morning of Easter Eve, to put out the earthly lights, and to await the coming of light from heaven[40] for the reception of which light one of the silver lamps, seven of which hang there, is prepared. Then all the clergy and people stand waiting with great and anx - ious expectation, until God shall send his hand down from on high. Among other prayers, they often shout loudly and with tears, "God help us!" and "Holy Sepulcher!"[41] Meanwhile, the patriarch or some of the other bishops who have assembled to receive the holy fire, and also the rest of the clergy, bearing a cross in which a large piece of our Lord's cross is inserted, and with other relics of the saints, frequently visit the Holy Sepulcher to pray there; watching also whether God has sent his gracious light into the vessel prepared to receive it. The fire has the habit of appearing at certain hours and in certain places; for sometimes it appears about the first hour, sometimes about the third, the sixth, or the ninth, or even so late as the time of compline.[42] Moreover, it comes sometimes to the sepulcher itself, sometimes to the Temple of the Lord, and sometimes to the Church of St. John. However, on the day when our humble selves, with the other pilgrims, were awaiting the sacred fire, immediately after the ninth hour that sacred fire came, upon which, behold, with ringing of church bells, the service of the Mass was said throughout the whole city, the baptismal and other services having been previously celebrated. As soon as the holy fire arrives, it is custom - ary to present it to the Temple of the Lord before anyone, except the patriarch, has lighted his candle at it.[43]

IX

THE CHAPELS OF ST. MARY AND OF THE HOLY CROSS, THE LORD'S PRISON, THE ALTAR OF ST. NICHOLAS, THE DOOR LEADING INTO THE CLOISTER

Upon the west side of the church, near the door, from which one mounts more than thirty steps from the church up to the street,[44] in front of the door itself, there is a chapel that is dedicated to Mary,[45] and which belongs to the Armenians. Also on the left side of the church, toward the north, there is a chapel dedicated to the holy cross,[46] in which is also a great part of the venerable wood itself, contained in a case of gold and silver; and this chapel is in the hands of the Syrians. Again, on the same side, opposite this chapel, toward the east, is a chapel of peculiar sanctity, in which there is a most holy altar dedicated to the holy cross. A large piece of the same blessed wood covered with gold, silver and jewels, is kept in a most beautiful case, so that it can be easily seen. When necessity requires it, the Christians carry this holy symbol against the pagans in battle. This chapel is also wonderfully decorated with mosaics. Heraclius, the Roman emperor, rescued this cross from Cosdre,[47] the king of the Persians, during the war that he waged with him, and restored it to the Christians.

Near this chapel, on the eastern side of it, one enters a dark chapel by about twenty steps, in which there is a most holy altar, under the pavement of which may be seen the mark of a cross.[48] In this place our Lord Jesus Christ is said to have been imprisoned[49] for a long time while he was waiting for Pilate's decision on the place of his passion, until his face was veiled and the cross erected on Calvary, so that he might be hung on it. Also, behind this chapel there is an altar dedicated to St. Nicholas.[50] Beyond this is the gate of the cloister through which one goes into the canons' cloister,[51] which stands round about the sanctuary. After one has made the circuit of the cloisters and is reentering the church from the other side of the door, one notices a figure of Christ on the cross[52] painted above the door of the cloisters so vividly as to strike all beholders with great remorse. Round it these verses are inscribed:

> You that this way do go,
> 'Twas you that caused my woe;
> I suffered this for you,
> For my sake vice eschew.

X

THE CHAPEL OF ST. HELENA,
THE GROTTO IN WHICH
THE CROSS WAS FOUND

To the eastward of this one goes down thirty steps and more to the venerable Chapel of St. Helena the empress, which is situated outside of the church itself, where there is a holy altar dedicated to her.[53] From here, again on the right hand, one descends fifteen or rather more steps into a subterranean cave, where on the right-hand corner of the cave one may see an open altar and beneath it a cross cut on the pavement, at which spot the empress is said to have discovered the cross of our Lord. There is an altar there dedicated to St. James. This chapel has no other window than the great opening in its roof.[54]

XI

THE CHAPEL OF THE FLAGELLATION,
THE TOMB OF DUKE GODFREY
AND OF THE KINGS OF JERUSALEM,
THE CHAPEL UNDER THE CAMPANILE,
THE CHAPEL OF JOHN THE BAPTIST,
AND ITS VICINITY

In another part of the church — that is to say, on the right hand, at the back of the choir — there is a fair altar, in which stands part of the column around which our Lord was tied and scourged.[55] Beyond this, on the south, be - fore the door of the church, may be seen five tombs,[56] of which the one nearest to the door, which is of white marble and costly skill, is that of the brother of the king of Jerusalem, named Baldwin; and the second one is that

of King Baldwin, the brother of Duke Godfrey, on which
is the following inscription:

> Here Baldwin lies, a second Judas Maccabee,
> His country's hope, the Church's pride and strength was he;
> Cedar and Egypt, Dan and Damascus insolent,
> Dreaded his might, and gifts and tribute humbly sent.
> Ah, well-a-day! he lies 'neath this poor monument.

The third tomb, beyond this, is that of his brother, Duke
Godfrey himself, who by his sword and his wisdom
recovered the city of Jerusalem, which had been invaded
by the Saracens and Turks, and restored it to the
Christians, replaced on the throne the patriarch who had
been driven out by the infidels, established a body of
clergy[57] in the church and settled endowments upon
them, that they might be strong to fight in God's cause.
The fourth tomb is that of the father[58] of the reigning
king, Amalric; the fifth is that of the father of the abbess
of St. Lazarus.

Also on the south there is a door, through which one
enters the chapel under the campanile; and from it one
passes into another chapel of great sanctity, dedicated to
John the Baptist, in which there is also a font. From there
one goes again into a third chapel. From the first chapel
one ascends to the street by forty steps or more.

XII

MOUNT CALVARY,
THE OUTSIDE VESTIBULE
BEFORE GOLGOTHA,
THE CHAPEL OF THE CRUCIFIXION,
THE CHAPEL OF GOLGOTHA,
THE DOOR OF THE CHURCH

It remains now to speak of Mount Calvary,[59] which shines in the church as does the eye in the head; from which by the death and blood-shedding of the Son of God, light and eternal life shall be poured forth for us. Before the entrance or door to the church, which is covered with solid bronze and is of a double form, one mounts by about fifteen steps to a small chamber, which is railed in and decorated with paintings. Here, at the top of the stairs, stand guardians watching the gate, who only allow as many pilgrims as they choose to enter, lest by excessive pressure, as often happens, there is crushing or danger to life. From that vestibule one ascends by three steps, through another door, into a chapel preeminent in sanctity and holiness beyond all other places under the sun.

This chapel is formed by four strong arches.[60] Its pavement is beautifully composed of various kinds of marble, and its vault or ceiling is most nobly decorated with the prophets — that is to say, David, Solomon, Isaiah, and some others — bearing in their hands texts referring to Christ's passion, wrought so beautifully on it in mosaic that no work under heaven could be compared with it, if only it could be seen clearly; for this place is somewhat darkened by the buildings around it. The place in which the cross stood on which the Savior suffered death is on the eastern side, raised on a high step covered on the left side with the finest Parian marble, and it displays a round hole almost wide enough to take in a person's head, in

19

which it is known that the cross itself was fixed. Into this hole pilgrims, out of the love and respect that they bear to him who was crucified, plunge their head and face.

On the right hand Mount Calvary itself, rising up higher, displays a long, wide, and very deep rift in the pavement, where the rock was rent asunder when Christ died. Yawning above and in front with a frightful cleft, it proves that the blood that flowed from Christ's side as he hung upon the cross found its way quite down to the earth. On the top of this rock it is customary for pilgrims to place the crosses that they have carried with them from their own countries; and we saw a great number of them there, all of which the guardians of Calvary burn in the fire on Easter Eve. In that chapel there is an altar of much sanctity, and on Good Friday the whole service for the day is celebrated at it by the patriarch and all the clergy.[61] On the wall on the left side of the altar there is a most beautiful painting of our Lord upon the cross, with Longinus standing on his right hand piercing his side with his spear; and on his left Stephaton offering him vinegar with the sponge and reed; with his mother also standing on his left hand, and St. John on his right; while two great scrolls, covered throughout with Greek inscriptions, are carried all around this work.

On the right hand also of the same altar a picture shows Nicodemus and Joseph taking down the dead Christ from the cross; where there is also the inscription, "The Descent of our Lord Jesus Christ from the Cross." From here one descends fifteen steps into the church and comes to that chapel that is called Golgotha, of great sanctity, but very dark. At the back of it is a deep recess, which enables the beholders to see the end of the cleft in the rock that came down from Calvary. In that place it is said that the blood of Christ stood after it had run down there through the cleft. Moreover above the arch that forms the boundary of Golgotha, or in other words, on the west side of Calvary, there is a picture painted on the wall, in which these verses[62] may be seen in golden letters:

> This place was hallowed by Christ's blood before,
> Our consecration cannot make it more;
> Howbeit, the buildings round this stone, in date
> Were on July the fifteenth consecrate
> By Fulcher patriarch in solemn state.

Outside the gate of the church, in the space between the two doors stands the Lord Christ in a saintly garment, as though just risen from the dead; while Mary Magdalen lies prostrate at his feet, but not touching them. The Lord holds out toward her a scroll containing these verses:

> Woman, wherefore weep'st thou,
>   kneeling unto him thou seekest dead?
> Touch me not, behold me living,
>   worthy to be worshipped.

XIII

THE CHAPEL OF THE THREE MARYS,
THE CHAPEL OF THE ARMENIANS,
ANOTHER LITTLE CHAPEL,
THE STREET AND MARKET,
THE CHURCH AND HOSPITAL OF
ST. JOHN THE BAPTIST,
THE CHURCH OF ST. MARY THE GREAT,
THE CHURCH OF ST. MARY THE LATIN

As one goes out of the church toward the south, one finds a sort of square courtyard paved with squared stone, on the left side of which, near Golgotha, on the outside, there is a chapel dedicated to the three Marys, which belongs to the Latins.[63] Further on toward the south there is another chapel, which is in the hands of the Armenians. Further on there is another little chapel. As one comes out of this open space, on the left there is a vaulted street full of goods for sale.[64] Opposite the church is the marketplace. Here, in front of the church, stand six columns,[65] with arches above them; and here, on the south side of the church, stands the Church and Hospital of St. John the Baptist.[66]

As for this, no one can credibly tell another how beautiful its buildings are, how abundantly it is supplied with rooms and beds and other material for the use of poor and sick people, how rich it is in the means of refreshing the poor, and how devotedly it labors to main - tain the needy, unless one has the opportunity of seeing it with one's own eyes. Indeed we passed through this palace and were unable by any means to discover the number of sick people lying there; but we saw that the beds numbered more than one thousand. It is not every one of the most powerful kings and despots who could maintain as many people as that house does every day; and no wonder, for, in addition to its possessions in other countries (whose sum total is not easily to be arrived at), the Hospitallers and the Templars have conquered almost all the cities and villages that once belonged to Judaea and that were destroyed by Vespasian and Titus, together with all their lands and vineyards. For they have troops sta - tioned throughout the entire country, and castles well fortified against the infidels.

Next to this to the east as one stands there, comes the Church of St. Mary, in which nuns, under the rule of an abbess, celebrate divine service daily. This place is said to have been dedicated to Mary because while our Savior was being maltreated on the way to his passion, she is said to have been shut up by his command in a chamber that then stood on that spot.

There closely follows another church on the east of this, which is also dedicated to our Lady,[67] because while our Lord was enduring such suffering for our salvation,

she fainted from excess of sorrow and was carried by
men's hands there into a subterranean grotto, where in the
indulgence of her grief she tore her hair from her head.
This hair is preserved to this day in a glass vessel in that
church. There is also in this church the head of St. Philip
the Apostle, lavishly adorned with gold; and the arm of
St. Simeon the Apostle, and the arm of St. Cyprian the
bishop. In this church monks serve God under a rule and
under the orders of an abbot.[68]

XIV

THE TEMPLE OF THE LORD:
THE COURTYARD, THE STAIRS,
THE SUBTERRANEAN GROTTO,
THE GREAT POOL, THE HOUSES,
THE GARDENS, THE SCHOOL OF ST. MARY,
THE GREAT STONE,
THE CLOISTER AND CONVENTUAL BUILDINGS
OF THE CLERGY,
AND OTHER POOLS

By a street[69] that bends a little toward the south through
the Beautiful Gate of the Temple one comes to the Temple
of the Lord,[70] crossing about the middle of the city;
where one mounts from the lower court to the upper one
by twenty-two steps, and from the upper court one enters
the Temple. In front of these same steps in the lower
court there are twenty-five steps or more leading down
into a great pool,[71] from which it is said there is a
subterranean connection with the Church of the Holy
Sepulcher, through which the holy fire that is miracu -
lously lighted in that church on Easter Eve is said to be
brought underground to the Temple of the Lord. In this
pool victims that were to be offered in the Temple of the
Lord were washed according to the precepts of the law.

Now, the outer court is twice as large, or more, than the inner court, which, like the outer one, is paved with broad and large stones. Two sides of the outer court exist to this day; the other two have been taken for the use of the canons,[72] and the Templars, who have built houses and planted gardens on them.

On the western side one ascends to the upper court by two ranges of steps, and in like manner on the southern side. Over the steps, before which we said that the pool is situated, there stand four columns with arches above them, and there, too, is the sepulcher of some rich man, surrounded by an iron grille, and beautifully carved in alabaster. On the right, also, above the steps on the south side, there stand in like manner four columns and on the left three. On the eastern side also there are fifteen double steps, by which one mounts to the Temple through the Golden Gate, according to the number of which the Psalmist composed fifteen psalms, and above these also stand columns. Besides this, on the south side above the two angles of the inner court, stand two small dwellings, of which the one toward the west is said to have been the school of the Blessed Virgin.[73] Now, between the Temple and the two sides of the outer court — that is the eastern and southern sides — there stands a great stone like an altar, which, according to some traditions, is the mouth of some pools of water that exist there; but, according to the belief of others, points out the place where Zacharias, the son of Barachias, was slain. On the northern side are the cloister and conventual buildings of the clergy. Round about the Temple itself there are great pools of water under the pavement. Between the Golden Gate and the fifteen steps there stands an ancient and ruined cistern in which in old times victims were washed before they were offered.

XV

THE DESCRIPTION OF THE TEMPLE:
THE PLACE WHERE CHRIST WAS PRESENTED
AND WHERE JACOB SAW THE LADDER

The Temple itself is evidently of an octagonal shape in its lower part. Its lower part is ornamented as far as the middle with most glorious marbles, and from the middle up to the topmost border, on which the roof rests, is most beautifully adorned with mosaic work. Now, this border, which reaches round the entire circuit of the Temple, contains the following inscription, which, starting from the front, or west door, must read according to the way of the sun as follows: On the front, "Peace be unto this house for ever, from the Father Eternal." On the second side, "The Temple of the Lord is holy; God cares for it; God hallows it." On the third side, "This is the house of the Lord, firmly built." On the fourth side, "In this house of the Lord all men shall tell of his glory." On the fifth, "Blessed be the glory of the Lord out of his holy place." On the sixth, "Blessed be they who dwell in thy house, O Lord." On the seventh, "Of a truth the Lord is in his holy place, and I knew it not." On the eighth, "The house of the Lord is well built upon a firm rock. "Besides this, on the eastern side opposite the Church of St. James, [74] there is a column represented in the wall in mosaic work, above which is the inscription, "The Roman Column."

The upper wall forms a narrower circle, resting on arches within the building and supports a leaden roof, which has on its summit a great ball with a gilded cross above it. Four doors lead into and out of the building, each door looking to one of the four quarters of the world. The church rests upon eight square piers and sixteen columns, and its walls and ceilings are magnifi-cently adorned with mosaics. [75] The circuit of the choir contains four main pillars or piers and eight columns, which support the inner wall, with its own lofty vaulted roof. Above the arches of the choir a scroll extends all round the building bearing this text: "'My house shall be called the house of prayer,' says the Lord. 'In it whoever asks, receives, and whoever seeks finds, and to anyone who knocks it shall be opened. Ask, and you shall receive; seek, and you shall find.'" In the upper circular scroll, similarly placed around the building, is the text: "Have thou respect unto the prayer of thy servant and to his supplication, O Lord, my God, that thine eyes may be open and thine ears turned toward his house night and day. Look down, O Lord, from thy sanctuary and from the highest heaven, thy dwelling place." (1 Kings 8:28-29.)

At the entrance to the choir there is an altar dedicated to St. Nicholas, set off in an iron enclosure, which has on its upper part a border containing this inscription in front: "In the year 1101, in the fourth indiction, Epact II," and on the left side, "From the taking of Antioch 63 years, from the taking of Jerusalem 53." On the right side, "From the taking of Tripoli 52 years, from the taking of Berytus 51 years, from the taking of Ascalon 11 years."

There is a place toward the east side of the choir that is surrounded by an iron enclosure with doors, which is worthy of the greatest reverence, seeing it was there that our Lord Jesus Christ was presented by his parents when he was brought to the Temple with an offering on the fortieth day after his birth. At the entrance of the Temple the aged Simeon took him in his arms and carried him to the place of presentation, in front of which these verses are inscribed:

The Virgin's child, the King of kings, was offered here;
This place we therefore deck with presents and revere.

Near this place, at scarcely a cubit's distance, is the stone that the patriarch Jacob placed under his head, on which he slept when he saw the ladder reaching up to heaven, by which the angels were ascending and descending, and said, "Truly the Lord is in this place and I did not know it." (Gen. 28:16.) In front of this place are the following verses:[76]

> Jacob, with his body resting, but with mind awake,
> Here saw the ladder, and his altar here did make.

XVI

THE CHAPEL OF ST. JAMES
OUTSIDE THE TEMPLE,
THE PLACE WHERE OUR LORD
WAS QUESTIONED ABOUT THE MIDDLE
OF THE WORLD,
WHERE EZEKIEL SAW THE WATERS,
THE CRYPT UNDER THE CHOIR,
THE WINDOWS, THE HIGH ALTAR,
THE HISTORY OF THE TEMPLE

From here, through the eastern gate, one enters the Chapel of St. James the Apostle,[77] the brother of our Lord, who was murdered by the impious Jews by being cast down from the the pinnacle of the Temple, and his skull broken with a fuller's club, and was first buried in the Valley of Josaphat near the Temple, but was afterwards translated here by the faithful with all honor, as became him, and placed in a sepulcher, above which is written the following epitaph:

> Say, stone and grave, what king's bones here find room?
> Saint James the Just: he lies within this tomb.

27

The chapel itself is round, being wide below and nar-row above, supported by eight columns, and excellently adorned with paintings. As we return from it by the same door, on the left hand, behind the jamb of the door, there is a place five feet in length and breadth on which our Lord stood when he was asked where he was in Jerusalem, which they assert is situated in the middle of the world, and he answered, "This place is called Jerusalem."[78] Behind the same door, opposite the just-mentioned place, that is, on the northern side, there is another place that contains the waters that the prophet Ezekiel saw flowing down from under the Temple on the right side (Ezek. 47:1-2).

As we return into the great church, on the south side near the choir, there is a door through which, down about forty-five steps, one enters the crypt, to which the Scribes and Pharisees brought the woman taken in adultery to the Lord Jesus and accused her, whose sins the holy master forgave and acquitted her. In memory of this indulgences are granted to pilgrims at this place. The church itself has thirty-six windows in its lower story and fourteen in its upper story, which added together make fifty, and is de-dicated to our Lady Mary, to whom also the high altar is consecrated. This church is said to have been built by the Empress St. Helena and her son the Emperor Constantine.

Let us consider how many times and by whom the Temple has been built or destroyed. As we read in the Book of Kings, King Solomon first built the Temple by divine command at a great expense — not in a round form as we see it today, but oblong (1 Kings 6:1-10). This tem-ple lasted until the time of Sedechia, king of Judah, who was taken by Nebuchadnezzar, king of Babylon, and led away captive into Babylonia, and with him Judah and Benjamin were also made captive and led away into the country of the Assyrians. Shortly afterwards his steward, Nabuzardan, came to Jerusalem with an army and burned both the Temple and the city; and this was the first destruction of the Temple. After seventy years of captivity the children of Israel returned to the land of Judah, led by Zorobabel and Esdras, by the favor and permission of Cyrus, the king of the Persians, and they rebuilt the same Temple in the same place and adorned it to the best of their ability. In rebuilding the Temple and the city they worked, it is said, holding a stone in one hand and a sword in the other, because of the continual assaults of the Gentiles who lived round about them. So, then, this was the second building of the Temple.

Afterwards the city, as may be read in the Book of Maccabees, though not entirely destroyed by Antiochus, king of Syria, was for the most part laid in ruins, the or - naments of the Temple utterly destroyed, the sacrifices forbidden, the walls broken down, and the Temple, as well as the city, made into a virtual wilderness. After this, Judas Maccabeus and his brethren, by God's help, put Antiochus to flight, drove his generals out of Judaea, and rebuilt and restored the Temple, replaced the altar and in - stituted the sacrifices and offerings by regular priests as of old. This was the third building of the Temple, and it remained until the time of Herod, who, Josephus tells us, although the Jews deny it, razed this Temple to the ground and built another greater one of more elaborate skill.

This was the fourth building of the Temple, which en - dured until the days of Titus and Vespasian, who took the whole country by storm and overthrew both the city and the Temple to their very foundations. This was the fourth destruction of the Temple. After this, as has been said a little way before, the Temple that we now see was built by the Empress Helena and her son the Emperor Constantine in honor of our Lord Jesus Christ and his holy mother. This, then, was the fifth restoration of the Temple.

XVII

THE PALACE OF SOLOMON,
THE HOUSE AND THE STABLE OF THE TEMPLARS
AND THEIR GARDENS,
THEIR STORES OF WOOD AND WATER,
THEIR GRANARIES AND REFECTORIES,
THEIR NEW AND OLD HALL,
AND THEIR NEW CHURCH

Next comes, on the south the Palace of Solomon,[79] which is oblong and supported by columns within like a church. At the end it is round like a sanctuary and covered by a great round dome, so that, as I have said, it resembles a church.[80] This building, with all its appurtenances, has passed into the hands of the Knights Templars. They dwell in it and in the other buildings connected with it and have many magazines of arms, clothing and food in it, and are ever on the watch to guard and protect the country. They have below them stables for horses built by King Solomon himself in the days of old, and adjoining the palace,[81] a wondrous and intricate building resting on piers and containing an endless complication of arches and vaults. This stable, we declare, according to our reckoning, could take in ten thousand horses with their grooms. No man could send an arrow from one end of their building to the other, either lengthways or cross - ways, at one shot with a Balearic bow. Above it abounds with rooms, solar chambers, and buildings suitable for all manner of uses. Those who walk upon the roof of it find an abundance of gardens, courtyards and antechambers, vestibules and rain-water cisterns; while down below it contains a wonderful number of baths, storehouses, gran - aries, and magazines for the storage of wood and other necessary provisions.

On another side of the palace, that is to say, on the western side, the Templars have erected a new building. I could give the measurements of the height, length and breadth of its cellars, refectories, staircases and roof, rising with a high pitch, unlike the flat roofs of that country, but even if I did so, my hearers would hardly be able to believe me. They have built a new cloister there in addition to the old one that they had in another part of the building. Moreover, they are laying the foundations of a new church of wonderful size and skill in this place, by the side of the great court.[82] It is not easy for anyone to gain an idea of the power and wealth of the Templars — for they and the Hospitallers have taken possession of almost all the cities and villages with which Judaea was once enriched, which were destroyed by the Romans, and have built castles everywhere and filled them with garrisons, besides the very many and, indeed, numberless estates that they are well known to possess in other lands.

XVIII

THE ANCIENT WALLS ROUND THE TEMPLE, THE RUINS OF ANTONIA, MORIA, THE CHURCH OF THE BATH OR OF THE MANGER OF OUR LORD, THE HOUSE OF SIMEON THE JUST

Now, the city wall on the southern and eastern sides sur - rounds all their dwellings, but on the west and the north a wall built by Solomon encloses not only their houses, but also the outer court and the Temple itself. On the north side of the court one wall and one gate remain entire among the ruins of Antonia that Herod built.[83] The hill itself on which the Temple stands was in ancient times called Moria,[84] and upon it David saw the angel of the Lord smiting the people with an unsheathed sword, when he said to the Lord, "I am he that have sinned: I have done wickedly. These that are the sheep, what have they done?

Let thy hand, I beseech thee, be turned against me, and against my father's house." (2 Sam. 24:17.) On this hill was the threshing floor of Araunah the Jebusite, which David bought from him to build a house for the Lord. Here by a postern there is a narrow way between the east - ern wall of the city and the garden of the Templars, whereby one comes to the most holy church, which is called the Church of the Bath or of the Manger of the Lord our Savior. In it the cradle of the Lord Christ is worshipped. This cradle stands in a place of honor at the east end on a high wall in front of a window. On the south side one sees a great basin made of stone lying on the ground, in which it is known that he was bathed as a child; and on the north side is the bed of our Lady, on which she lay while she suckled her child at her breast. One descends into this church by about fifty steps, and it once was the house of the just Simeon, who rests there in peace.

* *
*

PART II

XIX

THE BATHING POOL OF SILOE

As one goes southward from this church or from the angle of the city itself, down the sloping side of the hill along the outwork that the Templars have built to protect their houses and cloister, where also in ancient times the city itself stood, a little path leads to the bathing Pool of Siloe,[1] which we are told is so-called because the water of that fountain comes there by an underground course from Mount Silo. This appears to me to be doubtful, because our mount, on which the city stands, and several other mountains, lie between them, and no valley leads directly from the mountain to the pool, nor is it possible that there can be an underground passage through such great mountains because of the distance; for Mount Silo is two miles from the city. Therefore, without pronouncing any decision upon this point, let us tell our hearers what we know to be true. We declare it to be the truth that the water bubbles up out of the earth like a fountain and that after filling the pool and running down to another pool close by, it disappears.

One descends into the pool by thirteen steps, and round about it are piers bearing arches, under which a paved walk has been constructed all round it, made of large stones, upon which those who stand can drink the waters as they run down.[2] The second pool is square and sur -

rounded by a simple wall. This bathing pool was once inside the city, but it is now far outside it, for the city has lost almost twice as much in this direction as it has gained in the parts near the Holy Sepulcher.

XX

BETHANY, BETHPHAGE, THE GOLDEN GATE WITH ITS CHAPEL

Now, we ought to arrange the course of our account according to the passion of Christ, who by his grace permits us to partake of his sufferings that we may be able thereby to partake of his kingdom hereafter. A mile from Jerusalem is Bethany,[3] where stood the house of Simon the leper and of Lazarus and his sisters Mary and Martha, where our Lord was frequently received as a guest.[4] Bethany stands near the Valley of Olives, in which the mount ends toward the east. So on Palm Sunday our dear - est Lord Jesus Christ set out from Bethany, came to Bethphage,[5] which is half-way between Bethany and the Mount of Olives — and where now a fair chapel has been built in his honor[6] — and sent two of his disciples to fetch the ass and her colt. He stood upon a great stone that may be seen in the chapel and sitting on the ass went over the Mount of Olives to Jerusalem and was met by a great crowd as he descended the side of the mountain.

He went on, beyond the Valley of Josaphat and the Cedron Brook, until he arrived at the Golden Gate,[7] which is twofold. As he approached it one of the doors opened by itself, for the bolt fell out and violently drawing out its ring made the other door fly open with a loud noise. Therefore a chapel has been consecrated in honor of it, in which this ring, which is covered with gilding, is regarded with great reverence. The gate itself is never opened except on Palm Sunday and on the day of the Exaltation of the Cross,[8] because the Emperor Heraclius passed through it with a large piece of the wood of the cross that he had brought from Persia. Our Lord entered the Temple that same day and remained there teaching every day until the fourth day of the week.

XXI

PETER'S PRISON

With him, therefore, I wish to ascend on to Mount Sion and behold what he did after this; but, first, I wish to be imprisoned with Peter, that with him I may be taught by Christ not to deny him but to pray. On the way by which people go from the Temple to Mount Sion they pass a fair chapel. Here at a great depth beneath the earth, seeing that one descends twenty steps and more in order to enter it, is that prison in which Herod the younger bound St. Peter, and from which the angel of the Lord led him.[9] At the entrance of the chapel these verses are inscribed:

> Arise, put on thy cloak, Peter, thy chains are broke;
> Arise and leave this place, set free by heaven's grace.

> O now I know indeed from prison I am freed;
> Christ's love to me be praised, that me from bonds has saved.

XXII

MOUNT SION,
CHURCH OF ST. MARY,
THE PLACE WHERE SHE DIED,
THE ROOM OF THE LAST SUPPER,
WHERE THE HOLY GHOST CAME DOWN,
WHERE CHRIST WASHED THE APOSTLES' FEET,
WHERE THOMAS FELT THE LORD'S WOUNDS,
THE TOMB OF ST. STEPHEN

Mount Sion,[10] which stands to the south and is for the most part outside the city walls, contains the church dedi - cated to our Lady Mary.[11] This is well fortified with walls, towers and battlements against the assaults of the infidels, and here canons regular serve God under an abbot.[12] When you enter it you will find in the middle apse, on the left-hand side, the holy place at which our Lord Jesus Christ received the soul of his beloved mother, our Blessed Lady Mary, and raised it to heaven.

This work is square below and round above, sup - porting a dome. By about thirty steps on the right hand one mounts into the upper chamber,[13] which is situated in the extremity of the apse. Here may be seen the table at which our Lord supped with his disciples, and after the departure of the traitor gave to those disciples his mystical body and blood.[14] In the same upper chamber, at a distance of more than thirty feet to the south of that place, there stands an altar in the place where the Holy Ghost descended upon the Apostles. From here one de - scends by as many steps as one ascended and sees in the chapel beneath the upper chamber the stone basin, built into the wall, in which the Savior washed the feet of the Apostles. Here, close by on the right hand, there stands an altar in the place where Thomas felt the Lord's side after his resurrection, which for this reason is called the Altar of the Finger.

From this place one passes through a kind of ante -
room, a round sanctuary of the church, [15] and finds on its
left-hand side a holy altar, beneath which, without doubt,
the body of St. Stephen, the protomartyr, was buried by
John, bishop of Jerusalem. His body, we read in history,
was afterwards translated by the Emperor Theodosius
from Constantinople to Rome, having been first translat -
ed from Jerusalem to Constantinople by the Empress
Helena. Before the choir a column[16] of precious marble
stands near the wall, and simple-minded people like to
walk around it.

XXIII

THE CEDRON BROOK, GETHSEMANE, CHURCH OF ST. MARY, THE CHAPEL OF THE SEPULCHER, THE LITTLE CHAPEL ON THE STAIRS, THE LEGEND ABOUT A JEW WHO WISHED TO DRAG AWAY THE BODY OF THE BLESSED MARY

From here after his supper the Lord went out across the
Cedron Brook, where there was a garden. The Cedron
Brook passes through the middle of the Valley of
Josaphat. In the place where that garden was the Church
of St. Mary, with its conventual buildings, has been
founded, in which her own body was buried.[17] Through
a porch one descends by more than forty steps into a
crypt,[18] in which her holy sepulcher stands, covered with
most costly decorations of marble and mosaic work.[19] At
the entrance to this crypt these two verses are written:[20]

You heirs of life, come praise our Queen, to whom
Our life we owe, who has revoked our doom.

This sepulcher has twenty columns around it carrying arches, a border[21] and a roof above it. On the border itself are inscribed these verses:

> From hence, from Jos'phat's vale, a path leads to the sky!
> The Virgin here, God's trusting handmaid, once did lie;
> Spotless, from hence she rose, to her heaven's gate did ope,
> Poor sinners' Light and Way, their Mother and their Hope.

The roof has a round dome above it, supported by six pairs of columns, with a ball and cross above it, and between each pair of these little columns all around the dome there hangs a lamp. One enters the sepulcher from the western side and leaves it on the northern side. Her Assumption is excellently painted on the ceiling above, which contains this sentence under a straight line: "Mary has been taken up into heaven; the angels rejoice and bless our Lady, singing her praises." Around the sanctuary of the church itself also runs a scroll, containing this inscrip - tion: "The Holy Mother of God has been exalted to the Kingdom of Heaven, above the choir of angels." From here one ascends into the church by as many steps as one descended by into the crypt.

The church itself and all the conventual building con - nected with it are strongly fortified with high walls, strong towers, and battlements against the treacherous attacks of the infidels, and it has many cisterns around it. As one goes out of the crypt one sees a very small chapel placed on the steps themselves. In the church also the Syrians have an altar of their own. Also on the ceiling above the steps by which one descends into the crypt the Assumption of our Lady is shown in a painting, in which her beloved son, our Lord Jesus Christ, is present with a multitude of angels. Having received her soul, he bears it away into heaven, while the Apostles stand by in deep sor - row and devotedly minister to her. When her body is placed upon its most holy bier, a Jew is trying to pull away the covering that veils it, and an angel is cutting off both his hands with a sword. His hands are falling on the ground, and the stumps remain on his body. There is a tradition associated with this that when our Lady's soul had departed from her body on Mount Sion, as has been told in former chapters, the holy Apostles reverently placed her most blessed body upon a bier and were car - rying it along the road leading toward the east, outside the city wall, to bury it in the Valley of Josaphat. Now the Jews, among whom the burning hatred and envy with which they had so long persecuted her son was not yet ex - tinct, met it with the intention of offering some insult to it. One of them, bolder and unluckier than the rest, came up to the litter on which her holy body lay and endeavored with wicked audacity to tear away the veil that covered it. But the merits of the Blessed Virgin Mary and the vengeance of heaven severely punished his rashness, for both his hands and arms withered, which struck terror into the rest and made them flee swiftly away.

XXIV

THE CHURCH OF GETHSEMANE,
THE CHURCH OF THE PRAYERS
(OF OUR SAVIOR),
THE HIGH PLACE WHERE THE PATRIARCH
BLESSES THE PALM BRANCHES,
THE WAY BY WHICH
OUR LORD WAS LED CAPTIVE

As you journey from there southward toward the Mount of Olives, you meet with a church of no small size called Gethsemane,[22] which our Savior entered when he came out of the garden with his disciples and said to them "Sit here while I go forth and pray."[23] So as soon as you enter it you find a holy altar, and on the left hand you enter into a subterranean grotto and find four places marked, in each of which three of the Apostles lay and fell asleep. There is also on the left a great rock at the angle of the entrance to the grotto, upon which Christ pressed his fingers, leaving six[24] holes imprinted on it. A little higher up toward the Mount of Olives, he offered up three prayers in a place where now a new church is being built.[25] The place of one of these prayers is in the left-hand apse, that of another in the midst of the choir, and that of the third in the right-hand apse. In the space inter - vening between Gethsemane and the places of the prayers, on the side of the Mount of Olives where the crowds met our Lord with palm-branches, there is a high place built up of stones, where on Palm Sunday the palm branches are blessed by the patriarch. It was near these places that, while Jesus was trembling and falling, Judas came with lanterns and torches and arms, and the officers of the Jews arrested him, led him away, and brought him to the hall of the chief priest or of Caiaphas. After they had mocked him there all night, they brought him in the morning before Pilate, his judge.

XXV

THE PAVEMENT ON MOUNT SION,
THE CHAPEL OF OUR LORD
WITH THE COLUMN OF THE SCOURGING,
THE CHURCH OF GALILEE,
THE GROTTO INTO WHICH PETER FLED,
THE VIA DOLOROSA

After he had asked him many questions, Pilate caused him to be led to the judgment hall, and he sat down, by way of a judgment-seat, in the place that is called the Pavement,[26] which is situated in front of the Church of St. Mary,[27] on Mount Sion, in a high place near the city wall. Here is a holy chapel dedicated to our Lord Jesus

Christ, in which stands a great column round which the Lord was bound by Pilate and ordered to be scourged after he had been condemned by him to be crucified. There pilgrims are scourged in imitation of him. In front of the church, on a stone cut in the likeness of a cross, these words are inscribed: "This place is called the Pavement, and here the Lord was judged."

Beyond this, toward the east on the right hand, one descends from another part of the street down fifty steps to the church called Galilee,[28] where two links of the chain, with which St. Peter was bound, are kept. Further on, on the left-hand side of the altar, one descends by about sixty steps into a very dark subterranean grotto, into which St. Peter fled after his denial of Christ and hid himself in the corner of it. There he is depicted sitting, resting his head upon his hands, while he weeps over his holy master's sufferings and his own denial of him, while the servant-maid threateningly presses on him, and the cock stands and crows before his feet. This church is in the hands of the Armenians.[29]

From here our Lord was led around the city wall, where then there were gardens and now are houses, and was crucified.[30] For as the Apostle says, "Our Lord suffered outside the gate."

Now according to the best of our ability, we have told what we learned with our own eyes about Christ and his holy places. We shall now tell what is known about his friends and about other places. After this we shall tell of some things that we have seen ourselves and some that others told us of.

XXVI

THE PALACE OF PILATE,
THE CHURCH OF ST. ANNE,
THE POOL OF THE SHEEP-GATE,
THE CHURCH AND DWELLINGS
OF THE LEPERS,
THE GREAT CISTERN OF THE HOSPITALLERS,
THE CHURCH OF ST. STEPHEN,
THE HOSPICE AT THE GATE OF ST. LAZARUS,
THE CHURCH OF ST. CHARITON

By the side of the street that leads to the eastern gate near the Golden Gate, beyond the house or Palace of Pilate, which we have already said adjoins the same street, stands the Church of St. Anne,[31] the mother of our Lady Mary, to whose tomb one descends into a subterranean grotto by about twenty steps. There nuns serve God under the rule of an abbess. Whoever goes on to its northern side will find the Sheep Pool,[32] which lies in a deep valley near a rocky hill, crowned by some ancient building. This pool, as we are told in the Gospel, has five porticos, in the farthest of which stands the altar.

Whoever makes the circuit of the city walls, beginning the journey at the Tower of David, will find at the west - ern angle of the city the church and dwellings of the lepers, which are handsome and kept in good order. Passing by the great cistern of the Hospitallers, before you reach the northern gate,[33] you find upon a hill the Church of St. Stephen[34] the protomartyr who, when he was cast out of the gate and stoned by the Jews, saw the heavens opened in that place. In the midst of the city there is a place raised on steps enclosed by an iron railing, in the midst of which is a holy altar of a hollow form, which stands at the place where he was stoned, and where the heavens opened above him. This church is subject to the Abbot of the Church of St. Mary the Latin. At the gate itself stands a venerable hospice, which is called a *xenodochium* in Greek. When you have gone some dis - tance along this road,[35] taking the road to the left, toward the east, you will find a church belonging to the Armenians,[36] in which a saint named Chariton reposes, whose bones are covered with flesh, as if he were alive.

XXVII

THE MOUNT OF OLIVES,
THE CHURCH OF OUR SAVIOR
(OR OF THE ASCENSION),
THE LITTLE CHURCH OF ST. PELAGIA,
THE PATER NOSTER CHURCH

After this, as the time and hour of his Ascension was drawing near, our Lord climbed the Mount of Olives, stood there upon a great stone and, in the sight of his Apostles and graciously bestowing on them his blessing, ascended into heaven. Now the Mount of Olives, as we have already said, is the highest of all the mountains that surround the city. It abounds with fruits of all kinds, and contains on its topmost point a church of the highest sanctity dedicated to our Savior.[37]

One ascends into the church by twenty great steps; in the midst of the church there stands a round structure, magnificently decorated with Parian marble and bluo marble, with a lofty apex in the midst of which a holy altar is placed. Beneath this altar appears the stone on which the Lord is said to have stood when he ascended into heaven.[38] In the church divine service is performed by canons. It is strongly fortified against the infidels with towers both great and small, with walls and battlements and night patrols.

As one comes out of the church one comes upon a little church on its western side, which is dark, being in a subterranean grotto. When one has descended twenty-five steps into this, one beholds, in a large stone coffin, the body of St. Pelagia,[39] who ended her life immured there in the service of God. Also on the west side, beside the road that leads to Bethany, on the side of the Mount of Olives, there is a church of great sanctity[40] on the place where the Savior sat when he was asked by his disciples how they ought to pray, saying, "Our father, who art in heaven." This he wrote for them with his own hand. The writing is under the altar itself, so that pilgrims may kiss it. From the middle of the church a way also leads down about thirty steps into a subterranean grotto, in which the Lord is said to have often sat and taught his disciples.

* *
*

PART III

XXVIII

BETHANY,
THE CHURCH OF ST. LAZARUS,
THE CHURCH OF MARY AND MARTHA,
THE RED CISTERN WITH ITS CASTLE,
THE GARDEN OF ABRAHAM,
THE TOWERS AND HOUSE THERE

So having finished Jerusalem, which in my story has the same importance as the head has to the body, I must now put in the other places and, as it were, the limbs of this body.

Next comes Bethany,[1] which also is fortified not less by the nature of the ground than by the strength of the works there. Here is a holy double church, one part of which is glorified by the body of St. Lazarus, whom our Lord raised from the dead on the fourth day and who ruled the church at Jerusalem for fifteen years, the other by the remains of his sisters, Mary and Martha. Nuns serve God there under an abbess. Here our Lord and Savior was frequently entertained as a guest.

To the eastward, beyond Bethany, at a distance of four miles from Jerusalem, there stands on a mountain a Red Cistern, with a chapel attached to it. Into this cistern Joseph is said to have been thrown by his brothers.[2] Here the Templars have built a strong castle.[3] More than three miles further on is the Garden of Abraham, in a beautiful plain near the Jordan, half a mile from it. Its twofold extent[4] includes a great plain watered by a beautiful brook.

The width of the plain extends as far as the Jordan, and its length reaches down as far as the Dead Sea; it has soil fit for growing all manner of fruit, and it abounds in wood, which, however, is prickly like thistles. We saw the garden itself, full of trees bearing innumerable apples[5] but of a small size; and we also saw ripe barley there on the Monday after Palm Sunday.

Many towers and large houses are possessed there by the power of the Templars, whose practice, as also that of the Hospitallers, is to escort pilgrims who are going to the Jordan and to watch that they are not injured by the Saracens either in going or returning, or while passing the night there.[6]

XXIX

THE JORDAN,
THE MOUNT QUARANTANA,
THE FOUNTAIN OF ELISHA

A mile distant from here is the Jordan, which, running in a winding and twisting stream along the mountains of Arabia, pours itself into the Dead Sea and thereafter ap - pears no more. Between the Red Cistern and the afore - said valley lies a frightful wilderness, into which our Lord Jesus was brought that he might be tempted by the devil. At the end of this wilderness is a terrible mountain, very lofty, and so precipitous as to be almost inacces - sible,[7] which, while it rears its huge peak above, yawns with a deep and gloomy valley below. This place the laity call Quarantana,[8] and we may call Quadragena, because it was here that our Lord sat fasting for forty days and forty nights. The road to the place where our Lord sat goes along the middle of the mountainside, not straight, but made crooked by the irregularities of the ground, and, being everywhere slippery, in some places it forces pil - grims to crawl on their hands. At the top is a gate, and, when you have passed through it and proceeded a little way farther you will find a chapel built onto a grotto, made by human labor, and dedicated to our Lady. From here you ascend by a toilsome path that leads upward without any steps; passing over the huge and rugged clefts of the mountain, you enter another gate and by a path that bends back again twice, you gradually arrive at a third gate. Passing through this you will see a little altar dedi - cated to the holy cross, and, on the right hand of the little chapel that contains it, the sepulcher of a saint named Piligrinus,[9] whose hand, still covered with flesh, is shown there.

Now ascending by about sixteen steps to the top, you will find on the east side a holy altar, and on the west the holy place itself where our Lord sat, and, as we have al - ready said, fasted forty days and nights, and where, after his fast, angels ministered to him. This place is situated in the middle of the mountain, for its peak reaches upwards as far as its depth opens downwards.

On its summit may be seen a huge rock, on which the devil is said to have sat while he tempted him. From this mountain a view extends to a great distance beyond Jordan into Arabia, and even the frontier of Egypt be - yond the Dead Sea may be seen. The crest of Mount Quarantana and its subterranean caves are full of victuals and arms belonging to the Templars, who can have no stronger fortress or one better suited for the annoyance of the infidels.

As one ascends or descends this mountain, that is to say, at its foot, a great fountain[10] bubbles forth, which supplies the Garden of Abraham and the whole plain around it with water. There on the plain that is watered by the brook running from this fountain, pilgrims, as we have already said, pass the night, so that they may go on to Quarantana to pray and may wash themselves in the waters of the Jordan. They are protected on three sides by the garden itself from the ambushes of the infidels; on the fourth side they are guarded by patrols of the Hospitallers and Templars.

XXX

THE PLACE ON THE BANKS OF THE JORDAN WHERE OUR LORD WAS BAPTIZED, THE CHURCH AND CONVENT, THE CASTLE OF THE TEMPLARS, JERICHO, THE MOUNTAINS OF GILBOA

When our humble selves also had visited this place in order to pray there, desiring to wash in the waters of Jordan with the rest, we descended the mountain after sunset, just as darkness was coming on. Looking out from its heights over the flat plain below us, we saw, according to our reckoning, more than sixty thousand people stand - ing there, almost all of them carrying candles in their hands — all of whom could be seen by the infidels from the mountains of Arabia beyond Jordan. Indeed, there was a still larger number of pilgrims in Jerusalem who had recently visited this place.

In the very place where our Lord was baptized by John there is a great stone on which our Savior is said to have stood while he was being baptized, and thus the water of the Jordan came to him, but he did not enter it. On the very bank of the Jordan a church is built, in which six monks who inhabited it were beheaded by Sanginus,[11] the father of Noradin. There is here a strong castle of the Templars.

As you return by the direct path from the Jordan to Jerusalem, on the flat plain before you enter the mountain district, you come upon Jericho, past which flows a brook that runs down from the mountains of Jerusalem, and which is now reduced to a small town. It is, however, situated on fertile soil, where all fruits soon ripen. Many roses grow there that expand in a lavish abundance of petals. Thus the comparison, "Like a rose planted in Jericho," befits our Lady. It is also remarkable for large and excellent grapes. This place is under the jurisdiction of the Church of St. Lazarus in Bethany, but much of the land lies uncultivated on account of the inroads of the Saracens. To the north of this road, on the right hand, by the side of the aforesaid plain, the Mountains of Gilboa can be clearly seen.

XXXI

THE DESERT ELIM,
THE VALLEY OF MOSES,
THE MOUNTAINS OF SINAI, HOR, ABARIM,
AND THE MOUNT ROYAL,
THE PLACE WHERE THE CHILDREN OF ISRAEL
PASSED OVER THE JORDAN

The desert[12] through which the Lord once led the chil-dren of Israel, after they had come up from the Red Sea, lies between Egypt and Arabia. It was there that he fed them, as we read in the Bible with bread from heaven, and brought forth water out of the rock for them. But the desert in which the children of Israel found twelve wells of water and three-score and ten palm trees is on the borders of Arabia and is called Elim.[13] In Arabia, also, there is a valley, that is called the Valley of Moses,[14] because he twice struck the rock with his staff there and brought forth water from the rock for the people, from which fountain the whole land is now watered. In the same district is Mount Sinai, on which Moses fasted forty days and nights and also received the law written by the finger of God upon the stone tables. Mount Hor, upon which Aaron was buried, is in Arabia, as likewise is Mount Abarim, upon which the Lord buried Moses, whose tomb, however, is not to be found. There is also in Arabia a mountain that is called Mount Royal,[15] which Baldwin, king of Jerusalem, conquered in war and placed under the dominion of the Christians.

These are the boundaries and provinces through which the children of Israel passed when they came up out of Egypt and had passed over the Red Sea, slaying Sihon, king of the Emoreans, and Och, king of Basan, which countries lie between Idumaea and Arabia. They crossed the Jordan at the very place where Christ was baptized and, having taken Jericho on the plain, gained possession of the Promised Land, as we are told. At the time of the passage of the children of Israel, Arabia was so utter a wilderness that it had not even any distinguishing name.

XXXII

THE VALLEY OF ENNON NEAR JERUSALEM,
THE NEW CISTERN,
THE CHAPEL OF ST. MARY
WHERE SHE USED TO REST,
CHABRATHA — THE TOMB OF RACHEL

Whoever passes out of the western gate of the city near the Tower of David and follows a path toward the south will pass through the Valley of Ennon,[16] which skirts two sides of the city near the new cistern. At the distance of more than half a mile one will arrive at a chapel of special sanctity, dedicated to our Blessed Lady Mary, where she would often rest when she journeyed from Bethlehem to Jerusalem. At its door there stands a cistern,[17] at which passers-by refresh themselves. Beyond this is a field in which lie numberless heaps of stones, which the simple pilgrims delight in collecting there, because they say that on the Day of Judgment they will take their seats upon them. Close by is the place called Chabratha, where Rachel, the wife of Jacob, died after she had given birth to Benjamin. After she had been buried there Jacob piled up twelve stones over her grave, and now a pyramid stands there to which her name is attached.

XXXIII

BETHLEHEM, THE CHURCH OF ST. MARY, THE CHAPEL OF THE NATIVITY, THE MANGER, THE TOMB OF JOSEPH OF ARIMATHEA AND ST. JEROME, THE PLACE WHERE "GLORY TO GOD IN THE HIGHEST" WAS SUNG

Next comes the famous city of Bethlehem,[18] in which according to the predictions of the prophets, our dearest Lord Jesus Christ was born man, where there is a holy church[19] honored by the distinction of being a bishop's cathedral church. The high altar is dedicated to our Blessed Lady Mary. At the extremity of the right-hand apse, by the side of the door, one descends by twenty-five[20] steps into a subterranean grotto, where there is a holy altar of hollow form with a cross marked on the ground. This altar consists of four small columns, which support a large piece of marble. Upon this place are written the following two verses:

> Of angels virtues beyond compare
> A virgin here the very God did bear.

On the right hand, or toward the west, in this same cave one descends four steps and so comes to the manger, in which once not only lay hay for cattle, but where food for angels was found. The manger itself has been encased in white marble, with three round holes on the upper part, through which pilgrims offer to the manger their long-wished-for kisses.[21] This crypt is, moreover, beautifully decorated with mosaic work.[22]

Above the cave stands a holy chapel vaulted in a double form, in which, on the south side is a holy altar, and on the west the tomb of Joseph of Arimathea is shown in the wall. Not far from the manger of the Lord is the tomb of St. Jerome. His body is said to have been translated from here to Constantinople by Theodosius the Younger.[23] On the roof of the church itself a star of well-gilded copper glitters on the end of a lance, in allusion to the three Magi, who, as we read in the Gospel, came there by the leading of a star and, finding the child Jesus there with Mary his mother, adored him. A mile from Bethlehem the angel appeared to the shepherds, and the glory of the Lord shone around them. Here also appeared a multitude of the heavenly host, singing "Glory to God in the highest."

XXXIV

HEBRON, THE DOUBLE CAVE, THE RED EARTH, MAMBRE, THE OAK

Further on, toward the south, near the Dead Sea, is Hebron,[24] where Adam is said to have dwelt and been buried after he was driven out of Paradise.[25] This city was a city of priests in the tribe of Juda. It was also a dwelling place of giants and was in olden days called Cariatharbe,[26] or the "city of four," because four venerable patriarchs are buried there in a double cave[27] — that is to say, Adam, the first man created; Abraham,

Isaac, and Jacob, the three patriarchs; and their four wives, Eve, Sara, Rebecca and Lea. This city was before this named Arbe, and in its territory — that is, at its extremity — was a double cave looking toward Mambre, which Abraham bought for a price from Ephron, the son of Seor the Hittite. In the country near the city is found the red earth that is dug up by the inhabitants and eaten and exported to Egypt. Adam is said to have been made of this earth. Now, however much of this earth may be dug out in extent or depth, it is said to be restored the next year to as much as it was before by divine power.

Near this city is the mountain of Mambre,[28] at whose foot stands the oak that the moderns call *dirps* [29] beneath which Abraham beheld three angels and adored one and hospitably entertained them. This oak lasted until the time of the Emperor Theodosius, and from its trunk or root another has grown, which, although partly withered, still exists and is so wholesome that as long as a horseman holds a piece of it in his hands his horse will not founder.

Hebron was the first place reached by Caleb and Joshua and their ten companions, who were sent by Moses from Cadesbarne[30] to spy out the Promised Land. This city was afterwards the cradle of the kingdom of David, who by divine command reigned there for seven years.

XXXV

THE SEPULCHER OF LOT, LAKE ASPHALTITES, SEGOR, THE STATUE OF SALT, CARNAIM

Two miles from Hebron was the sepulcher of Lot, Abraham's nephew. Ten miles from Hebron, toward the east, is Lake Asphaltites, which is also called the Dead Sea,[31] because it receives into itself nothing living, or the "Sea of the Devil," because at his instigation the four cities of Sodom, Gomorra, Seboim, and Adima went on in their wickedness and were burned with fire of brimstone from heaven and were sunk in this lake, which rose in the place of the aforesaid cities. The water of this pool is shocking from its hideous color, and its stench drives away those who approach it. Once a year, on the anniversary of the destruction of those cities, stones and wood and things of other kinds are seen to float on the surface of the lake, in testimony of their ruin.[32]

Near the lake is the city of Segor, which is also called Bala and Cara, which was saved from destruction by the prayers of Lot and remains to this day. As Lot went out of it his wife looked back and was turned into a statue of salt, which endures to this day and which, as it grows smaller when the moon is waning, so also increases in size when she waxes and has its face turned behind its back. This lake also produces bitumen, which is called Jews' pitch and is of great use to sailors. Round about its banks is likewise found alum, which the Saracens call *katranum.* Above the lake, as one goes down to Arabia, is the city of Carnaim, on the mountain of the Moabites, upon which Balac, the son of Boer, the king of the Moabites, placed Balaam, the seer, to curse the children of Israel. This mountain, on account of its precipice, is called "Cut off." This lake divides Judaea from Arabia.

XXXVI

GAZA, ASCALON, JOPPA, ARIMATHEA, THE FIELD OF ABACUC

Ten miles westward from Hebron, on the shore of the Mediterranean Sea, stands Gaza, which is now called Gazara, where Samson did many great deeds and carried away its gates by night. Eight miles from Gaza, on the shore of the Mediterranean Sea, is Ascalon,[33] a very strongly fortified city. These cities used to stand in

Palestine, or, rather, in the country of the Philistines. On the shore of the same Mediterranean Sea is Joppa, where the Apostle Peter raised Tabitha from the dead and which the moderns call Jafis. Near it is Arimathea, from which came Joseph, the noble counselor[34] who buried Christ. There also, that is in the land of Juda, is the field where Abacuc the prophet was carried off by an angel when he had kneaded bread in a trough and was going into the field to take it to the reapers, and was carried away to Babylon, that he might take food to Daniel in the den of the lions.[35]

XXXVII

THE CHARNEL-HOUSE OF THE LION
NEAR JERUSALEM

As you go out of the Holy City, toward the west by the gate near the Tower of David, on the right hand there is a path that leads to a chapel, in which one descends by about one hundred steps into a very deep subterranean cave and finds the bodies of numberless pilgrims, which are said to have been brought there in the following manner. All the pilgrims who came one year to pray as usual found the city full of Saracens. Being unable therefore to enter it, they besieged those who were in the city. But, as they had neither food nor arms sufficient for accomplishing of so arduous a feat, they began to be in great straits for want of provisions. While they were thus in want, the Saracens, seeing that they were unable to resist, suddenly sallied forth from the city and put them all to the sword. Now, as a stench arose from the corpses of so many people, they determined to burn them all; but that same night a lion appeared, sent from God, who cast all the bodies into that cave, which has a narrow mouth. Every particle of them may be carried across the sea; indeed, when it is put on board, the ships are said to go home of their own accord.[36]

XXXVIII

THE CHURCH OF THE HOLY CROSS, THE PLACE IN THE WOOD OR OF ST. JOHN, THE MOUNTAINS OF MODIN OR BELMONT, EMMAUS OR FONTENOID, THE MOUNTAINS OF SOPHIM, RAMATHA, BETHORON, SILO OR THE MOUNTAIN OF THE HOLY SAMUEL

Next, beyond a certain mountain, follows a most fruitful and beautiful valley, in which stands a noble church dedicated to our Lord Jesus and to his beloved mother. There under an open altar people worship the holy place in which stood the trunk of the tree from which was cut the cross on which the Savior hung for our salvation. This church belongs to the Syrians and is strongly fortified with towers, walls and battlements against the treacherous attacks of the infidels. It is, moreover, a - dorned with houses, dining rooms, chambers and dwell - ings of all kinds suitable for all kinds of uses, raised high aloft in stonework. This tree is said to have been cut down by King Solomon, who marked it with the figure of the cross and put it away in a fitting place to await the coming of the Savior, because he foresaw in the spirit that salvation would be brought to the world through Christ's death.[37]

From there one passes on to St. John's, or to the place that is called "In the Wood," where his father Zacharias and his mother Elizabeth lived, and where St. John him - self was born, where also Mary, after she had received the salutation of the angel at Nazareth, came and saluted St. Elizabeth. Near this place are the mountains of Modin, upon which Mathathias sat with his sons when Antiochus took the city and the children of Israel by storm. These mountains are called by the moderns Belmont.

Near these mountains is the castle of Emmaus,[38] which the moderns called Fontenoid, where the Lord appeared to two of his disciples on the very day of his resurrection. Not far from here are the mountains of Ephraim, which are called Sophim; and soon comes Ramatha, a great city, which is now called Rames, of which Helchana, the father of the prophet Samuel, and Anna, his mother, were natives. Near Sophim is Bethoron, which now is called Beter. On the right hand, or western side of that district, two miles from Jerusalem, one ascends Mount Silo, from which springs of sweet water flow into the valleys beneath it. There[39] the Ark of the Covenant of the Lord remained from the entry in the children of Israel into the Promised Land until the time of Heli the priest. In his time the ark was forced by the sins of the Hebrews to be captured by the Philistines and kept by them until, struck by a scourge from heaven, they placed the same ark on a wagon and unwillingly brought it back to Bethsames seven months after it had been captured. Here, as the anger of the Lord raged fiercely against both the priests and the people because they had kept the ark, the men of Cariathiarim,[40] or Gabaa, came and took it away from Bethsames and kept it in their own country. Afterwards King David and all Israel brought it away with singing and hymns of praises and deposited it in the City of David on Mount Sion. After this, when King Solomon had built the Temple of the Lord, as aforesaid, he placed the ark in the Temple on Mount Moria, where the threshing floor of Areuna the Jebusite had been. In Silo, also, the prophet Samuel was buried. Thus changing its former name, the place was called St. Samuel's, and there dwells a convent of professed monks called gray monks.[41]

XXXIX

LYDDA, CACHO, CAESAREA OF PALESTINE, MOUNT CAIPHA (CARMEL) AND THE TOWN

Six miles to the west of Silo, on the plain, is Lydda,[42] the burial place, according to tradition, of St. George the Martyr. Therefore the place has lost its ancient name and is called St. George's by the moderns. From here one goes down by the way that leads toward Achon, or Ptolemais, through a pleasant and beautiful plain that extends between the mountains and the flat country by the seashore, on which are many cities and towns, both new and old. Among these are Caphar Gamala, Caphar Semala, a fortress that the moderns call Cacho, which is situated in a very fertile valley, the fortified town, which is now called Caesarea of Palestine[43] and was once called the Tower of Strato,[44] and the Mountain of Caipha,[45] near which stands a half-ruined town of the same name.

Here it is said that the thirty pieces of silver were made that were given to the traitor Judas as the price of the blood of Christ. On the top of the mountain there is a castle of the Templars, which enables mariners to recognize the mainland from a distance.[46]

XL

THE NEW CASTLE OF ACCARON, THE GROVE OF PALMS, PTOLEMAIS

Further on by the seashore, opposite Accaron, a great castle of that name stands in a rich country and is called the New Castle.[47] Near it is a very large grove of palm trees, and three miles further on is Ptolemais itself,[48] a great, rich, and populous city. However, the harbor or roadstead of Ptolemais is difficult and dangerous to access when the wind blows from the south and the shores tremble under the continual shocks that they receive from the waves and are there heaped into great masses. For, since the fury of the sea is not broken by the intervention of any mountain, the terrible waves boil over more than a stone's throw onto the land.[49] In this city the Templars have built a large house of admirable skill by the seashore, and the Hospitallers likewise have founded a stately house there.

Wherever the ships of pilgrims may have landed them, they are all obliged to repair to the harbor of this city to take them home again on their return from Jerusalem. Indeed, in the year when we were there — on the Wednesday in Easter week — we counted eighty ships in the port besides the ship called a "buss," on board of which we sailed there and returned.[50] Along the road that leads from Jerusalem through the aforementioned places to Ptolemais one meets with many deserted cities and castles, which were destroyed by Vespasian and Titus; but one also sees very strongly fortified castles, which belong to the Templars and Hospitallers.

XLI

THE LITTLE CHURCH AT THE SPOT FROM WHICH PILGRIMS FIRST SEE JERUSALEM, THE VILLAGE OF MAHUMERIA AND THE CHURCH OF ST. MARY, ANOTHER VILLAGE, SICHEM OR NEAPOLIS, THE SARACENS

Two miles from the Holy City, on the northern side, there is a little church at the place where pilgrims, filled with great joy at their first sight of the city,[51] lay down their crosses and take off their shoes and humbly strive to seek him who deigned, for their sakes, to come there poor and humble. Three miles from here is a large village called Mahumeria[52] by the moderns, where close by a church dedicated to Mary stands a great cross of hewn stone, raised on seven steps. These steps are climbed by pilgrims, who from here, and not without groans, see the Tower of David standing, as stated above, on Mount Sion at a distance of more than four miles. The old name of this village has escaped my memory.

Eight miles from here another great village stands on a lofty mountain height, from which, by a precipitous path, one descends through a beautiful and boundless plain and over some other mountains to a very strongly fortified city, which in ancient days was called Sichem, or Sichar, but now is called Neapolis,[53] or the New City. As we passed along this road we were met by a multitude of Saracens, who were proceeding with bullocks and asses to plough up a great and beautiful plain, and who, by the hideous yells that they thundered out, as they usually do whenever they set about any work, struck no small terror into us. Indeed, numbers of infidels dwell there through - out the country, as well in the cities and castles as in the villages, and they till the earth under the safe conduct of the king of Jerusalem or that of the Templars or Hospitallers.[54]

XLII

SICHEM AGAIN,
THE WELL AND CHURCH OF JACOB,
CAIN AND ABEL,
THE TEREBINTH OF RACHEL,
BETHEL OR LUZA,
MOUNTS GERIZIM AND EBAL

The aforementioned city of Neapolis is situated in Samaria and abounds in springs and rivers, vineyards, olive groves, and trees of all kinds, while its soil is fertile and excellently cultivated.[55] When our Lord Jesus came here, weary with his journey, he sat down beside the spring where he talked with the woman of Samaria. Now, the well upon which our Lord sat is half a mile from the city and stands in front of the altar in a church, which has been built over it, in which God is served by nuns. This well is known as Jacob's Well[56] and stands on the land that he gave to his son Joseph. This city was once destroyed by the sons of Jacob, who slew Sichem, its prince, the son of Hamor the Hivite, because he had ravished Dinah, their sister. This city stands between Dan and Bethel, and in it Jeroboam, king of Israel, made two golden calves, of which he set up one in Dan and the other in Bethel. Near Sichem are two mountains; one, on which Cain is said to have offered sacrifice to God of the fruits of the earth, dry and desolate; the other, on which Abel likewise offered sacrifice to God of the fatlings of his flock, rich in trees and plentiful in fruits of all kinds. To Sichem were brought the bones of Joseph from Egypt, and near it is the terebinth beneath which his mother Rachel hid the idols that she had stolen from Laban, her father.[57]

A mile to the east is Bethel, which before was called Luza, where Isaac's sacrifice by his father Abraham took place, and where also Jacob, sleeping with his head laid upon a stone, beheld the ladder reaching up to heaven and the angels of God ascending and descending by it, and the Lord himself standing above the same. Close by one sees Mount Gerizim over against Mount Hebal,[58] from which Moses ordained that the people should be blessed or cursed as they deserved.

XLIII

SAMARIA OR SEBASTE,
THE CRYPT OF HELISAEUS AND ABDIA,
THE SEPULCHERS OF THE SEVENTY PROPHETS

Six miles from here is Samaria,[59] also called Sebaste, which the moderns call St. John's and which stands on a strong though not high mount. From it the province of Samaria itself has received its name, and its great ruins give it the appearance of a city. It is rich in its soil and plenteous in vineyards and all fruits.[60] In this place the disciples of St. John the Baptist[61] buried the body of their master, after his head had been cut off by Herod the Younger in the castle of Machaerunta, as a present for a dancing girl. It is said to have been afterwards burned by Julian the Apostate. His head, however, was first carried to Alexandria, was translated from there to an island called Rhodos,[62] and was afterwards removed by the Emperor Theodosius to Constantinople. Moreover, a piece of his arm is preserved there and is held most sacred. He was buried in the crypt between the prophets Helisaeus and Abdia, in the cave in which that prophet once fed seventy prophets, who are also buried there. One goes into it down thirty-five steps.

XLIV

GINAEA, JEZRAHEL,
THE MOUNTAINS OF GILBOA,
SCYTHOPOLIS, THE CASTLE OF SAPHAM,
MOUNT HERMON,
ANOTHER CASTLE

Ten miles from here is the town of Genin,[63] at which place Samaria begins. Five miles from Genin is Jezrahel,[64] which is now called *Ad Cursum Gallinarum.* Here dwelt Naboth, who was stoned for the sake of his vineyard by that impious woman Jezabel, whom after - wards Jehu caused to be trampled by his horses' feet there. Near Jezrahel is the field of Mageddo, where Ozias, king of Juda, was conquered and slain by the king of Samaria. Many ruins of this city are still to be seen, as also a pyramid called by the name of Jezabel. A mile from Jezrahel to the east are seen the mountains of Gilboa. Two miles from it stands the city that once was called Bethsan,[65] or "The House of God," and which is now called Scythopolis, on whose wall we read that the heads of Saul and of his sons were hung when the strang - ers (Philistines) had slain them in war. This city marks the eastern border of Galilee, whose capital it is.

In its neighborhood, on a lofty mountain, the Hos - pitallers have built a very strong and spacious castle,[66] so that they may protect the land on this side of the Jordan against the treacherous attacks of Noradin, the despot of Aleppo.[67] There is also close by, on the west, a castle of the Templars named Sapham, strongly fortified to repel the inroads of the Turks. Beyond this, toward the Medi - terranean, is Mount Hermon, at the foot of which, on the west side, the Templars have built a castle of no small size, in whose grounds they have made a large cistern with a wheeled machine for drawing water.[68]

XLV

TIBERIAS,
THE PLACE CALLED THE TABLE,
THE SEA OF GALILEE,
THE MOUNTAIN ON WHICH OUR LORD
USED TO PASS THE NIGHT,
PANEAS OR BELINAS, JOR AND DAN,
THE JORDAN, THE PLAIN OF MEDAN,
THE VALLEY IN THE FIELDS

Beyond this come the most beautiful and most fertile plains, at the end of which, toward the north, stands the city Tiberias on the Sea of Galilee, where our Lord satisfied five thousand people with five loaves and three fishes.[69] Therefore this place is called the Table, and traces of the miracle may be seen there to this day. Near, also, is the place where the Lord appeared to his disciples after his resurrection and ate part of a fish and honey - comb in their presence. Here is the Sea of Galilee on which our Lord, walking, came to his disciples about the fourth watch of the night. Then, as Peter walked on the waves and was beginning to sink, he took him by the hand and said, "Thou of little faith, why didst thou doubt?" (Matt 14:31.) Here also, at another time, when his disciples were in danger, he made the sea quiet. Near the same sea, not far from Tiberias, is that mountain to which, seeing a multitude, he ascended. On it he often sat and addressed his disciples and the people, and on it he used to pass the night. Here also he deigned to heal the leper.

At the foot of Mount Libanus, which is the boundary of Galilee toward the north, is the city of Paneas,[70] which after being rebuilt by Philip, the tetrarch of Ituraea and the region of Traconitis, was called Caesarea Philippi in memory of his own name and likewise in honor of Tiberius Caesar, under whom he governed. This city, which is called Belinas by the moderns, was rescued from the infidels in the year 1161 after the incarnation of our Lord Jesus Christ by the Christians, who have established a garrison of their own people in it.[71] In this country two springs, that is, Jor and Dan, both rise, which flow separately as far as the mountain of Gibel and from there form the Jordan.[72]

The Jordan, as has been said in former chapters, flows from the Gibel Mountains to Lake Asphaltites through the valley that is called "The Great Valley" or "The Valley of the Meadows," which is bounded on both sides by a con - tinuous chain of mountains from Libanus to the desert of Pharan.[73] Its course divides Galilee from Idumaea and the land of Bosra, which is the second capital of the Idumaeans, next to Damascus. Dan from its source flows underground as far as the plain named Medan, where it displays its channel quite openly.[74] An innumerable mul - titude of people assemble on this plain every year at the beginning of the summer, bringing with them all manner of things for sale, and with them come a vast number of Parthians and Arabs to protect the people and their flocks, which remain in those parts throughout the summer. After leaving this plain, Dan passes through Sueta, in which the monument of the blessed Job still exists and is held sacred by the inhabitants. From there it flows toward Galilee of the Gentiles to the city of Cedar, passes by the plain of thorns,[75] where the medicinal places are, and joins the Jor. The Jordan, however, flows out of the lake far away from Paneas and, after passing between Bethsaida and Capharnaum through the Sea of Galilee, makes a fresh start.

XLVI

BETHSAIDA, CEDAR, CHORAZAIN, CAPHARNAUM, BETHULIA, THE LAKE OF GENNESARETH, MAGDALUM, CINNERETH (TIBERIAS), MOUNT TABOR, NAIN, ENDOR

This is Bethsaida[76] to which Peter and Andrew, John and James, the son of Alphaeus belonged. Four miles from Bethsaida is Chorazain, in which it is believed that Antichrist will be born, because the Lord rebuked them, saying, "Woe to thee, Chorazain! Woe to thee, Bethsaida!" Five miles from Chorazain is Cedar, a fine city, of which the prophet says in the Psalm, "I dwell amid the tents of Cedar." (Ps. 120:5.) Capharnaum, also on the right-hand side of the same sea, is the city of the centurion whose child our Lord raised from death. Four miles from Tiberias is the city of Bethsaida, from which Judith came who slew Holofernes. Four miles from Tiberias, toward the south, is Dothaim, where Joseph found his brethren. On the left-hand side of the same sea, in the hollow of a mountain, the little plain of Gennesareth juts out. Since it is surrounded by hills on all sides and feels no wind that blows, it is said to make a wind for itself by the emission of its own breath. Two miles from Gennesareth is the town Magdalum, from which came the Magdalen. This province is called Galilee of the Gentiles and belongs to the tribes of Zebulon and Nephthalim.

In the upper parts of this Galilee are the twenty cities that King Solomon is said in the Book of Kings (1 Kings 9:11) to have given Hiram, king of Tyre. Two miles from Magdalum is Cinereth, which is also called Tiberias, of which we have already spoken. Five miles to the west of Tiberias is Mount Tabor[77] of great height, on which our Lord Jesus Christ was transfigured in the presence of his disciples. On this mountain a glorious church has been built and dedicated to the Savior, in which monks serve God under an abbot.[78] It is said that the service of the Mass was celebrated for the first time in this church. On the skirts of this mountain Melchisedech, the priest of the most high God and king of Salem, met Abraham as he was returning from the slaughter of Abimelech and offered him bread and wine.[79]

Two miles from Tabor is the city of Nain, at whose gate our Lord raised up the widow's son from death and restored him to her.[80] Above Nain is Mount Endor, at whose foot, on the banks of the Cadumin Brook, which is the Cison Brook, Barach, the son of Abinoem, acting on the advice of Deborah the prophetess, triumphed over Jabin, king of the Idumaeans, and Sisara, the captain of his host, pursued Zeb and Zebee and Salmanna, the kings of the Ismahelites, Agarenes, Amalechites and Amonites, across the Jordan, and on his return from pursuing them found Sisara himself slain by Jahel, the wife of Heber the Cinaeite, with a nail driven through his temple into the ground.[81]

XLVII

NAZARETH, THE CHURCH OF ST. MARY, THE GROTTO OF THE ANNUNCIATION, THE TOMB OF JOSEPH, THE BIRTHPLACE OF THE BLESSED MARY, THE MIRACLE WROUGHT AT THE FOUNTAIN OF GABRIEL, THE PLACE OF THE CASTING DOWN

Four miles from Tabor toward the west, on the road that leads to Accon,[82] stands the most glorious city of Nazareth, in which there is a venerable church, which enjoys the honor of being the cathedral church of a bish - op, and which is dedicated to our Blessed Lady Mary.[83]

In the left-hand apse of this church one descends by about fourteen steps into a subterranean grotto, in which at the east end there is a small cross marked on the ground beneath an open altar, which marks the place at which the angel Gabriel delivered the message of Christ to our Lady.

On the left hand of this altar, that is, to the north, her husband St. Joseph, who brought up the Savior, lies buried. Over him is placed an altar. On the right hand, that is, on the south side, there is a place with a small cross marked on the ground and arched above, in which the Blessed Mother of God came forth from her mother's womb at her birth. All men tell of a great and wondrous miracle about this city that, whenever the infidels attempt to attack it, they are stricken with blindness or some such plague from heaven and are forced to desist.

A fountain in this city flows forth through a sprout fashioned in marble like the mouth of a lion,[84] from which the child Jesus often used to draw water and take it to his mother. This fountain is said to derive its origin from the following events. Once when the boy Jesus came to draw water from the cistern his pitcher was broken by his comrades in their play, and he drew the water and carried it to his mother in the lap of his tunic. She refused to drink it, since he did not seem to have brought it in a sufficiently clean manner. As if in a rage, he flung it out of his lap on to the ground and from the place where it fell the fountain that still flows is said to have burst forth. A mile to the south of Nazareth is the place called the "Place of the Casting Down," because the Jews wished to cast Christ down when he passed through the midst of them and went his way.

XLVIII

SEPPHORIS, CHANA OF GALILEE, THE CASTLE OF THE TEMPLARS, PTOLEMAIS, THE ROAD THAT LEADS FROM THERE TO JERUSALEM BY THE MOUNTAINS, AND THE ROAD THAT LEADS TO JERUSALEM BY THE SEASIDE

Two miles from Nazareth is Sepphoris, [85] a fortified city on the road to Accon. From here came the blessed Anne, the mother of the mother of Christ. Four miles from Nazareth, two miles from Sepphoris toward the east, is Chana[86] of Galilee, from which came Nathanael and Philip, and where our Lord turned water into wine. Also three miles from Sepphoris on the road to Accon is a very strong castle of the Templars,[87] and a little more than three miles further is Accon, or Ptolemais, itself. Now, this road that leads from Accon through Nazareth, Samaria and Neapolis to Jerusalem is called the Upper Road; and the one that leads from Accon through Caesarea and Lydda to Jerusalem is called the Seaside Road.

XLIX

DAMASCUS, HUS, SUETA, THEMAN, NAAMAN,
ARPHAT, AMAT, SEPHARNAIM,
THE JABOK BROOK, MOUNT SEIR,
THE PLACE WHERE SAUL WAS CONVERTED
INTO PAUL,
THE RIVERS PHARPHAR AND ABANA,
THE PLAIN ARCHAS, ANTIOCH

Arabia joins Idumaea in the district of Bosra. Idumaea is
a province of Syria.[88] Damascus is the chief city of the
Idumaeans and is the city that Eliazar, the servant of
Abraham, built in the field in which Cain slew his brother
Abel. In Damascus once lived Esau and Seir and Edom,[89]
after whom all that land is called Idumaea. A part of it is
called Hus, from which came the blessed Job; and a part
also is called Sueta,[90] from which was Baldach[91] the
Suite. In this same province is the city of Theman, from
which came Elephat[92] the Themanite. There also is the
city of Naaman, from which came Zophar the
Naamathite. Arphat[93] and Amat and Sepharnaim are
cities of Damascus.

In the country of the Idumaeans, two miles from the
Jordan, runs the Jabok Brook. After he had forded it on
his return from Mesopotamia, Jacob wrestled with an
angel who changed his name from Jacob to Israel. In
Idumaea is Mount Seir, upon which stands Damascus.
Two miles from Damascus is the place where Christ over -
threw Saul and raised up Paul, making a friend out of an
enemy and a teacher of the truth out of a persecutor of it.
At the foot of the mountains of Libanus rise Pharphar and
Abana, the rivers of Damascus, of which one, namely
Abana, runs through the plain of Archas[94] and empties
into the Mediterranean Sea. Into those parts St.
Eustachius retired after the loss of his wife and sons.
Pharphar runs through Syria to Antioch, flows beneath its

walls, and ten miles away from the city pours into the Mediterranean Sea at the port of Solim,[95] which is called the Port of St. Simeon. In this city St. Peter first obtained the pontifical dignity, and it is still the seat of a patriarch.

L

PHOENICIA, THE METROPOLIS, MAMISTRA, ANTIOCHIA, TRIPOLIS OR TURSOLT, GIBELETH, BERYTUS, THE WONDERFUL IMAGE THERE

Libanus divides Phoenicia from Idumaea. The city of Tyre is the chief city of the province of Phoenicia, whose inhabitants, the Syrians say, refused to receive Christ when he walked by the seashore, but he himself said that he was only sent to the lost sheep of the house of Israel. The following are the great walled cities by the sea that, being in Syria, the province of Palestine and Judaea, are subject to the dominion of the Christians: Mamistra and Antioch, and Tripolis, which is called Tursolt by the moderns, and the city that contains the very strong castle that is called Gibeleth,[96] are cities of the province of Coele Syria.

Next, to the south, on the seashore, comes Berytus, called by the moderns Baruth,[97] a rich and strong city, large and populous, in which the Jews, the enemies of the cross of Christ, once crucified an image of him thinking to offer an insult to him. After they had done all the shameful deeds that they had learned that their fathers did to Christ on the cross, they even pierced the side of the image with a spear, and when blood and water flowed forth, even as it did from Christ when he hung on the cross, adding sin to sin they caught it in vessels and dared to tempt[98] God. But almighty God turned their evil into good; for since they would have had even more cause to hate him if the effects of divine virtue had not resulted from it, they anointed the limbs of cripples with the same blood, and seeing that those who were anointed with this sacred fluid immediately recovered their health, they bent their necks to the profession of the Christian faith.[99] This figure is to this day preserved as a sacred relic in the church of that city, which is eminent as being the cathedral church of a pope.[100]

LI

SIDON, SAREPTA, TYRE, THE CASTLE SCANDALIUM, THE CASTLE OF IMBERTUS, PTOLEMAIS AND THE OTHER CITIES BY THE SEASIDE

Sixteen miles from Berytus is Sidon, a noble city, from which came Dido, who founded Carthage in Africa. Six miles from Sidon is Sarphan, which is also called Sarepta of the Sidonians,[101] in which the widow fed Helias the prophet, and in which also by means of the same prophet, God raised the widow's son, that is the prophet Jonah, from the dead.

Eight miles from Sarphan is Tyre,[102] which the moderns call Sur, which stands by the seashore and surpasses all the other cities in the strength of its towers and walls. The city is quadrangular in shape and presents the appearance of an island. Nearly three of its sides are surrounded by the sea; the fourth is very strongly fortified with ditches, barbicans, towers, walls, battlements, and loopholes.[103] It has only two entrances, which are guarded by quadruple gates with towers on either side. It is remarkable, like Accon, for having a double harbor. In the inner harbor are moored the ships of the city and in the outer one those of foreigners.

Between the two harbors two towers, built of great masses of stone, project into the sea. Between them, as a gate, stretches a huge chain made of iron. This gate, when closed, renders entrance or exit impossible but permits them when open. This city is honored by being the seat of a bishop.[104]

Four miles from here is a castle named Scandalium,[105] through which waters that rise above it run in their down - ward course to the sea at that place. Three miles from there is a large village, which is called by the moderns the Castle of Imbertus.[106] Four miles further comes Accaron or Ptolemais, and three miles further Old and New Caipha. Sixteen miles further is Caesarea of Palestine, which, with the harbor that adjoins it, was splendidly built by King Herod. Also fourteen miles further is Joppa or Jafis, with a harbor that is dangerous to shipping in southerly gales. Beyond these, in order, are Gaza or Gazara and the very strong fortress of Ascalona, all of which have been described already. All these cities are on the seacoast, and all of them are large and enclosed by walls.

This account of the holy places, wherein our Lord Jesus
Christ appeared in bodily presence, having taken on
himself the form of a servant for our sake, we
have put together partly from what we have
ourselves seen, and partly from what we
have heard from the truthful reports of
others, in the hope that the minds of
those who read or hear it may be
roused to love him through
their knowledge of the
places that are
described
here.

*

CHURCH OF THE HOLY SEPULCHER

THE SOUTH FACADE FROM THE PARVIS c. 1486

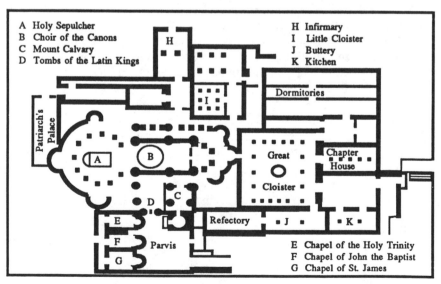

A Holy Sepulcher
B Choir of the Canons
C Mount Calvary
D Tombs of the Latin Kings

H Infirmary
I Little Cloister
J Buttery
K Kitchen

E Chapel of the Holy Trinity
F Chapel of John the Baptist
G Chapel of St. James

PLAN c. 1175

NOTES

Part I

1. The Mediterranean. See map, p.xx.

2. Mount Seir or Edom.

3. The position of Ramathaim is uncertain; but the place long pointed out as Samuel's Tomb is the height most conspicuous of all in the neighborhood of Jerusalem immediately above the town of Gibeon, known to the Crusaders as "Montjoye," since it was the spot from which they first saw Jerusalem, called *Neby Samwil,* the Prophet Samuel, at the turn of the century. See chaps. 38 and 41, pp. 57, 59 below; "Samuel," in *Harper's Bible Dictionary,* ed. Madeleine S. Miller and J. Lane Miller, 8th ed., New York: Harper & Row, 1973, p. 641.

4. Probably the Tomb of Absolom. See Jerome Murphy-O'Connor, *The Holy Land,* Oxford and New York: Oxford University Press, 1986, p. 103; *Encyclopedia of Archeological Excavations in the Holy Land,* ed. M. Avi-Yonah and E. Stern, 4 vols., London: Oxford University Press, Englewood Cliffs, New Jersey: Prentice-Hall, 1975-78, 2: 601, 629-30.

5. The Valley of Hinnom or Gehinnom. See below, chap. 32, pp. 50-51.

6. See chap. 4, p. 7.

7. The Benedictine house. See Prawer, pp. 171, 178; *Encyclopedia of Archeological Excavations* 2: 626.

8. This is probably that on the north wall outside St. Stephen's Gate. See *Encyclopedia of Archeological Excavations* 2: 624.

9. This is the Golden Gate. See chap. 20, pp. 34-35.

10. On population, topography, trade, housing and sanitation, see Hazard, pp. 9-13; Peters, pp. 295-311.

11. The Phasael Tower, originally dating from Herod's reign. See Murphy-O'Connor, pp. 24, 92; *Encyclopedia of Archeological Excavations* 2: 599, 604-26; Hazard, p. 33; Prawer, pp. 323-24, 435.

12. New St. Mary, the Nea. See Murphy-O'Connor, p. 71. *Encyclopedia of Archeological Excavations* 2: 617, 625.

13. See *Encyclopedia of Archeological Excavations* 2: 590.

14. Or Aceldama. See Murphy-O'Connor, p. 95; see also chap. 3, p. 5 above.

15. Fabri, who was in Jerusalem in A.D. 1483, says that there was once a church in the field of Aceldama, which was built by the Empress Helena and dedicated to All Saints. Felix Fabri, *Wanderings in the Holy Land*, trans. Aubrey Stewart, London: Palestine Pilgrims' Text Society, 1892-93; reprint ed., New York: AMS, 1971, 8: 534-35. See Prawer, p. 209.

16. 1 Kings 1:33-34. Gihon on the Ophel ridge. See Murphy-O'Connor, pp. 96, 100.

17. The house stood to the west across the Sheep Pool from St. Anne's on Jehoshafat Street. See *Encyclopedia of Archeological Excavations* 2: 624.

18. See Hazard, pp. 91-92; *Encyclopedia of Archeological Excavations* 2: 607.

19. See Murphy-O'Connor, p. 32 and his map on p. 30.

20. See Hazard, pp. 74-84; *Encyclopedia of Archeological Excavations* 2: 626; Prawer, pp. 422, 424-28, 431-37, 452-54; Peters, pp. 311-14. The present church differs significantly. For a description of the site following the fire of 1808 and the earthquake of 1927, see Murphy-O'Connor, pp. 43-51.

21. Compare the account given in *The Pilgrimage of the Russian Abbot Daniel in the Holy Land*, C.W. Wilson, ed., London: Palestine Pilgrims' Text Society, 1895; reprint ed., New York: AMS, 1971, chap. 10, pp. 12-13. On the standard pilgrim's itinerary, see Hazard, pp. 58, 75-76.

22. What is now shown as the Stone of Unction is opposite the door of the church. The first one appeared in the 12th century. The present one dates from 1810. See Murphy-O'Connor, p. 49.

23. See Hazard, p. 118.

24. The present tomb is described as a "hideous kiosk." See Murphy-O'Connor, p. 49.

25. John of Würzburg (chap. 12, pp. 37-38) says "silver." See the Preface to the First Edition, above p. xvi.

26. See Abbot Daniel, Appendix 2, pp. 91-92.

27. Probably the work of the Emperor Manuel Comnenus. See John of Würzburg, chap. 12, p. 36; and Phocas, chap. 14, pp. 19. See also Hazard, p. 78.

28. Actually 18 pillars. The plan may have involved alternating piers and columns. See Hazard, pp. 76-77; Prawer, p. 427.

29. Hazard, p. 117.

30. On the south side. The ancient Christian practice of separating men and women in church is carried out in this mosaic.

31. The old Roman robe of state.

32. The Choir of the Canons, or *Chorus dominorum*, is evidently the translation of the German *Domherrenchor*. "King Godfrey also instituted canons with prebends and gave them habitations round a - bout the church." William of Tyre 9.9: "*In Ecclesia Dominici Sepul - chri sunt Canonici Sancti Augustini, qui habent Priorem, sed soli*

Patriarchae obedientiam promissunt. " See *Brocardi Descriptio Ter -rae Sanctae,* A.D. 1230; Prawer, pp. 426-28; Hazard, pp. 76-78.

33. See chap. 11, pp. 17-18.

34. See Hazard, pp. 117-18. *Celatura.* Stewart found under the word "ceeling with syllure" in the *Promptorium Parvulorum,* ed. Albert Way, 1865, the following note: "The Catholicon explains *celo* to signify *sculpere, pingere,* and *celamen* or *celatura* sculpted or painted decoration. Lydgate, in the *Troye Boke,* uses the word *celature* to describe vaulted work of an elaborate character. It appears doubtful whether the verb "to cele," and the word "ceiling," which is still in familiar use, are derivable from *coelo,* or may not be traced more directly to *coelum* and the French *ciel,* signifying not only vaulting or ceiling, but also the canopy or *baldaquin* over an altar; the hangings or estate over a throne that are sometimes called *daïs,* from the throne being placed in that part of an apartment to which that name properly belonged; and lastly, the canopy of a bed, "celler for a bedde, *ciel de lit.*"

35. In his note to this passage Tobler remarks that there is in the Bavarian National Museum at Munich an ivory carving of the fourth century, on which Christ is represented in precisely this attitude.

36. Compare Fabri, 8: 425.

37. The altar, which is described here, is that of the *compas* or center of the earth. See John of Würzburg, chap. 11, p. 34, and note. Possibly Theoderich confused his cicerone's account of this altar with that of the altar in the Angel Chapel. What is now shown as the Stone of Unction and mentioned by Fabri (8: 373-74) and other writers, stands in another part of the church. Innominatus 7 (p. 70), says, "To the eastward of the sepulcher, in the midst of the choir, is the middle of the world, where the Lord was laid when Nicodemus took him down from the cross." On Jerusalem as the navel, or center of the earth, see Prawer, p. 428; Wright, pp. 259-60; Eliade, pp. 42-45.

38. The Jacobites ("a familiar sound," says Gibbon, writing in 1788, "which may startle an English ear") were so called after James Baradaeus, or Zanzalus, who reorganized the sect of the Monophysites, or believers in the unity of the human and divine natures of Christ. On the Jacobites in the Crusader Kingdom, see Runciman, 2: 135-36, 322-23 *et passim*; Prawer, pp. 53-54, 220-21 and 228-29.

39. Copts.

40. See Abbot Daniel (chap. 97, pp. 74-80), for references to authorities on the subject of the holy fire. See Peters, pp. 259-67, 523-24, 571-78, *et passim.*

41. The war cries of the Crusaders.

42. Compline was sometime between 6:00 and 8:30 pm. For a brief explanation of the medieval hours, see David Knowles, *Christian Monasticism,* New York: McGraw-Hill, 1969, pp. 212-23.

43. See John of Würzburg, chap. 13, p. 38, n. 2; Abbot Daniel, chap. 92, p. 78, note.

44. This obviously indicates the raising of the level of the medieval city above that of ancient Jerusalem. The famous Christian sites would have remained in constant use by pilgrims and other devout, while the strata of the intervening millennium raised the street level. For the facade, see Hazard, pp. 78-79; Prawer, pp. 431-37.

45. St. Mary of Egypt. See Hazard, p. 79.

46. Hazard, p. 79.

47. Chosroes II, who took Jerusalem in 614, completing his conquest of Syria. The True Cross was restored by his son Kavad II (Siroes) in 628 after Chosroes' murder.

48. This probably means "in the pavement under which," etc.

49. The prison is in the northeast corner of the church. See Hazard, p. 79.

50. Apparently on the site of the modern Chapel of St. Longinus. See Tobler.

51. On the east side of the church. See Murphy-O'Connor, p. 51; Hazard, pp. 79-80.

52. See Hazard, p. 118.

53. See Hazard, pp. 77, 80.

54. At the eastern end of the church. John of Würzburg (chap. 13, pp. 38-39), alludes to these two chapels. Theoderich, Tobler tells

us, is the first writer who distinctly describes the Chapel of the Invention of the Cross. See Murphy-O'Connor, p. 51 ; Hazard, p. 77, plan.

55. This column is mentioned by Saewulf (*Saewulf*, trans. Canon Brounlow, London: Palestine Pilgrims' Text Society, 1892; reprint ed., New York: AMS, 1971, p. 11), A.D. 1102, before the Crusaders' church was built. See Willis, *Church of the Holy Sepulchre*, London: J. Parker, 1849, p. 92, note. It is shown at the present day in the Chapel of the Apparition, in which services are held according to the Latin rite. See Fabri 8: 349. This chapel is in the southeast corner of the church to the right of the entrance. Murphy-O'Connor, p. 48.

56. Stewart discusses these in his Preface, pp. xv-xvi above. These tombs were under the Greek chapel just north of the Latin chapel. The tombs of Godfrey and Baldwin were removed by the Greeks in 1809. See also Hazard, p. 90.

57. See chap. 7, p. 13.

58. King Fulke, the father of Baldwin III and Amalric. The fifth tomb was that of Baldwin II, whose daughter Judith was abbess of the convent of St. Lazarus of Bethany. His eldest daughter, Queen Milicent, married Fulke of Anjou, who was the ancestor of the English Plantagenet kings.

59. In the southeast section of the church behind the Greek chapel.

60. For a description of the chapel, see Hazard, pp. 79, 81, 118, 318, pl. xxx.

61. On the Easter and Ascension liturgy, see Prawer, pp. 178-82.

62. These verses, with the exception of the last one, are quoted by John of Würzburg, chap. 13, p. 39.

63. Tobler tells us that the Chapel of St. John the Baptist and of Mary Magdalen were in the west side of the forecourt. We must look for the Chapel of the Three Marys, that of the Armenians and the "other little chapel upon the east side." See Hazard plan, p. 77.

64. The Covered Street. See *The City of Jerusalem* in *The City of Jerusalem and Ernouls' Account of Palestine*, trans. C.R. Conder, London: Palestine Pilgrims' Text Society, 1896; reprint ed., New York: AMS, 1971, chap. 16, p. 18.

65. Their appearance, with the arches above them, probably resembled that of the existing arcade at the entrance to the Haram area. On this and Jerusalem's other markets, see Prawer, pp. 409-10; *Encyclopedia of Archeological Excavations* 2: 624.

66. See John of Würzburg, chap. 5, p. 21. Hazard, pp. 37, 54, 84; Peters, pp. 324-27.

67. St. Mary the Latin. See Hazard, pp. 84-85; *Encyclopedia of Archeological Excavations* 2: 626; Prawer, pp. 170, 178, 209.

68. For the position of both of these convents see Williams' *Memoir on Jerusalem*, London, J.W. Parker, pp. 17, 18; and Tobler's elaborate note on this passage. See also his note on Innominatus 1, chap. 2, p. 2. The first is the Church of St. Mary the Great. The second is St. Mary the Latin. Its site is now occupied by the late 19th century Church of the Redeemer. On St. Mary the Great, see *Encyclopedia of Archeological Excavations* 2: 624, 627; Prawer, pp. 170-71; Hazard, pp. 84, 270-71.

69. Possibly the Temple Street, leading from the Vegetable Market and the Covered Street past the Latin Money Exchange. See *Encyclopedia of Archeological Excavations* 2: 624.

70. The Dome of the Rock, the former Mosque of Omar, on the site of the Temple of Solomon. See Prawer, pp. 94, 171, 209, 418-19; Hazard, pp. 86-90, 272-73; *Encyclopedia of Archeological Excavations* 2: 590, 604-6, 623-24, 626; Peters, pp. 316-20; Murphy-O'Connor, p. 73-86.

71. *In Templo Domini Abbas est et Canonici regulares. Et est scien - dum, quod aliud est Templum Domini, aliud Templum militiae, illi clerici sunt, isti milites. Brocardi Descriptio Terrae Sanctae*, A.D. 1230. See *Encyclopedia of Archeological Excavations* 2: 623-24.

72. This account agrees materially, though not in detail, with that given by John of Würzburg, chap. 4, pp. 12-20.

73. See *Encyclopedia of Archeological Excavations* 2: 624.

74. The little mosque now called the Kubbet es-Silsile, or "Dome of the Chain" (see Edrisi 5), was called the Chapel of St. James (Jacob) by the Crusaders. See *Encyclopedia of Archeological Excavations* 2: 623-24; Hazard, p. 86; Murphy-O'Connor, p. 80.

75. See Murphy-O'Connor, pp. 78-79.

76. These lines appear to be an incorrect version of those given by John of Würzburg, chap. 4, p. 14. They are quoted in nearly the same words as John by Innominatus 7, p. 71.

77. St. James the Less. See above, p. 25 and n. 74.

78. This is probably the "pierced-rock" that marked the site of Solomon's Temple and the Rock of Mohammed's Ascension. For medieval Christians the actual *omphalos,* or center of the world, was marked by a cross in the pavement of the Choir of the Canons of the Holy Sepulcher. See above p. 14, n. 37; Peters, p. 274, photo.

79. The Al-Aqsa Mosque. See Prawer, pp. 39, 97, 171, 176, 178; Peters, pp. 320-24; *Encyclopedia of Archeological Excavations* 2: 623-34. Jacques de Vitry writes, "There was also another immense temple besides the Dome of the Rock, located to the southeast of it, and from this Temple of Solomon, not from the Temple of the Lord, the Templars took their name." *History of Jerusalem,* bk. 1.

80. See the translation of Procopius, *De aedificiis,* in the Palestine Pilgrim's Text Society series, bk. 5, chap. 6, and Appendix 1; also John of Würzburg, chap. 5, pp. 20-21.

81. John of Würzburg (chap. 5, p. 21) declares that these stables could hold more than two thousand horses or fifteen hundred camels. See *Notes to the Ordnance Survey of Jerusalem; Encyclopedia of Archeological Excavations* 2: 623-24.

82. See John of Würzburg, chap. 5, p. 21, n. 2. This church was destroyed by Saladin.

83. Murphy-O'Connor, p. 32 and map p. 30; Hazard, p. 91; *Encyclopedia of Archeological Excavations* 2: 607.

84. See *Encyclopedia of Archeological Excavations* 2: 580.

Part II

1. See Murphy-O'Connor, pp. 101-2. On the important pilgrim sites around Jerusalem see Hazard, pp. 55-56; Prawer, pp. 204-13.

2. See the Bordeaux Pilgrim, *Itinerary from Bordeaux to Jerusalem (333 AD)*, trans. Aubrey Stewart, London: Palestine Pilgrims' Text Society, 1887; reprint ed. New York: AMS, 1971, Appendix 3.

3. Murphy-O'Connor, pp. 115-18.

4. See John of Würzburg, chap. 6, p. 22; Prawer, pp. 172, 210. He does not mention any church or convent at Bethany. We know, however, that there was a convent at Bethany dedicated to St. Lazarus, of which Judith, one of King Fulke's daughters, was abbess. See Theoderich chap. 11, p. 18, and chap. 28, pp. 45-46. There was a Church of St. Mary Magdalen in Bethany, which once had been the house of Simon the Leper. See Tobler's note.

5. Murphy-O'Connor, p. 114-15.

6. On its frescoes see Hazard, pp. 123, n. 9, 261-62. John of Würzburg says (chap. 6, p. 24): "Between this Bethany and the top of the Mount of Olives, about half-way was Bethphage, a village of priests, traces of which still remain in two stone towers, one of which is a church."

7. Murphy-O'Connor, pp. 83-84; Hazard, p. 83, n. 6; *Encyclopedia of Archeological Excavations* 2: 623.

8. September 14.

9. Probably St. Peter in Chains. John of Würzburg (chap. 16, pp. 46-47) describes this chapel and tells us that he celebrated mass there on St. Peter's Day (August 1). He quotes the verses without any variation. See Murphy-O'Connor, p. 66, fig. 20(T), and p. 72.

10. Murphy-O'Connor, pp. 92-95; *Encyclopedia of Archeological Excavations* 2: 580-96; Hazard, p. 57.

11. The Nea Church. See Murphy-O'Connor, p. 71; *Encyclopedia of Archeological Excavations* 2: 617, 627; Prawer, p. 178.

12. *In ecclesia Montis Sion est Abbas et Canonici regulares.* He was a mitred abbot. *Brocardi Descriptio Terrae Sanctae*, A.D. 1230.

13. See Hazard, p. 95. Compare the descriptions given by John of Würzburg (chap. 7, p. 25); the *City of Jerusalem* (chap. 1, p. 2); the Abbot Daniel (chap. 41, pp. 36-37); and Phocas (chap. 14, p. 18).

14. Murphy-O'Connor, pp. 93-94; Hazard, p. 67.

15. Hazard, pp. 95, 262-63.

16. Murphy-O'Connor, p. 71.

17. North of the Garden of Gethsemane. A Benedictine abbey and rule with "Cluniac influence." See Hazard, pp. 96-97, 110, 114; Murphy-O'Connor, pp. 108-9.

18. Hazard, p. 97, gives 48.

19. See Hazard, p. 97.

20. These and the following verses are quoted by John of Würzburg (chap. 18, p. 52).

21. *Limbus*. This word is used very loosely by our author. Here it seems to mean a "tambour" extending around the church above the arches and carrying the upper range of columns with the dome.

22. The village of Gethsemane is mentioned by Abbot Daniel (chap. 20, pp. 22-23), and John of Würzburg (chap. 18, p. 53). No trace of it remained in Stewart's day. The site of the Garden of Gethsemane is presently covered by the Church of All Nations. See Murphy-O'Connor, pp. 107-9. See also Hazard, p. 55, for its place in the pilgrim's itinerary; for general descriptions, see pp. 96-97; *Encyclopedia of Archeological Excavations* 2: 626-27.

23. Mark 14:32.

24. John of Würzburg (chap. 8, p. 27) says "five."

25. This account reads as though there were two churches. John of Würzburg (chap. 8, p. 27) speaks only of the Chapel of Agony and the "new church enclosing the place where our Lord prayed in whose flooring stand out three unwrought stones," etc. See Hazard, p. 97.

26. Tobler's admirable note makes it abundantly clear that in the time of Theoderich, in the last days of the Frankish kingdom of Jerusalem, the house of Pilate, the Praetorium, and the prison had been confused with one another. Here Theoderich follows the west - ern of the routes introduced by the Latins, as opposed to the one to the north of the Temple or the eastern route, where the Via Dolorosa now begins. See Murphy-O'Connor, pp. 33-34; Hazard, p. 95.

27. The Nea Church. See Murphy-O'Connor, p. 71; p. 76, n. 12 above.

28. It was also called "Gallicantus," or "In Gallicantu," though this name properly belonged to the Grotto of the Cock-crowing within the church. Abbot Daniel (chap. 42, p. 37) says that thirty-two steps led down to this grotto. See John of Würzburg, chap. 9, p. 29. This church is possibly to be identified with the Ramban Synagogue. See Murphy-O'Connor, p. 72. See also Hazard, pp. 95, 272 and 294.

29. John of Würzburg (chap. 9, p. 29) calls them Greeks.

30. The chief authorities will be found in the *Harper's Bible Dictionary*, article on "Jerusalem," pp. 314-21. See also Murphy-O'Connor, pp. 33-34.

31. Still intact. See Murphy-O'Connor, pp. 29-31; Hazard, pp. 73, 93-94, 271-72.

32. The Pool of Betheseda. See Hazard, p. 94.

33. St. Stephen's or the Damascus Gate.

34. Northwest of the city outside St. Stephen's Gate or the Damascus Gate. See Abbot Daniel, Appendix 1, pp. 83-90. For the frescoes there, see Hazard, pp. 262-63.

35. See John of Würzburg, chap. 16, p. 48.

36. John of Würzburg (chap. 16, p. 48) calls the "Syrians."

37. *In ecclesia Montis Oliveti est Abbas et monachi nigri. Brocardi Descriptio Terrae Sanctae*, A.D. 1230. He, as well as the Abbot of Mount Sion of the Temple, was a mitred abbot. For a description of the church, see Hazard, pp. 97-98.

38. Hazard, p. 97.

39. The legend of St. Pelagia is recounted by Fabri 8: 499-500.

40. The shrines of the Paternoster and Credo. Hazard, p. 97.

Part III

1. See above, pp. 34-35; Hazard, pp. 98, 261-62; Murphy-O'Connor, pp. 115-18.

2. John of Würzburg (chap. 2, p. 7) places this cistern on the plain of Dothaim, between Genon and Sebaste, or Samaria.

3. Tobler has an interesting note on this passage. He is unable with certainty to identify this site with that of the Templars' Bourg Maledoin, which may either have been here or on the summit of Quarantana.

4. The text here seems to be corrupt.

5. A vague term for fruit of all kinds.

6. Tobler conjectures that here occurs a considerable lacuna in the text.

7. It was for the purpose of defending the pilgrims down these passes that, in 1118, the nine knights banded together who formed the nucleus of the Order of the Templars. See Stanley's *Sinai and Palestine*, chap. 7, p. 314. For bibliography on the Templars, see Prawer, pp. 550-51; and Desmond Seward, *Monks of War,* Frogmore, England: Paladin, 1974.

8. The Mount of Quarantine. See Hazard, pp. 59, 379.

9. The Latin word *pelegrinus,* "pilgrim," strongly implies that this was the tomb of some anonymous pilgrim.

10. The fountain of Elisha. "No one," says Mr. Grove, "who has visited the site of Jericho, can forget how prominent a feature in the scene are the two perennial springs, which, rising at the base of the steep hills of Quarantana behind the town, send their streams across the plain towards the Jordan." See "Elisha" in *Harper's Bible Dictionary*, pp. 159-60; Hazard, p. 59. 2 Kings 2:15-19.

11. "Zenghi (1127-45) proved his first arms against the Franks in the defeat of Antioch. Thirty campaigns in the service of the caliph and sultan established his military fame....After a siege of twenty-five days, he stormed the city of Edessa and recovered from the Franks their conquests beyond the Euphrates. The corruption of his name into *Sanguin* afforded the Latins a suitable allusion to his

sanguinary character and end: *'Fit sanguine sanguinolentus.'* William of Tyre, 16. 4, 5, 7." See also Gibbon, chap. 59, 6: 349; Runciman 2: 181-84, 194-98, 203-5, 215-19, 225-28, 233-39, 241-44 *et passim.*

12. Here begins the "old compendium," which is copied by Theoderich, John of Würzburg (chap. 22, p. 61), and Fetellus with great uniformity. Theoderich resumes his personal narrative with the words, "These are the boundaries," in chap. 32.

13. Exod. 15:27.

14. Wady Mousa.

15. Montréal. Built by Baldwin I in 1115, about 18 miles from Petra. See Hazard, p. 149; Prawer, pp. 50; 131; 146, n. 22; 282.

16. Hinnom or Gehinnom. See chap. 3, pp. 5-6.

17. The Birket es Sultan. See Tobler's note.

18. Murphy-O'Connor, pp. 165-71. For Bethlehem's place in the medieval itinerary, see Hazard, pp. 58-59.

19. The Church of the Nativity. See Murphy-O'Connor, pp. 167-71. See Stanley's *Sinai and Palestine*, chaps. 14, 32, p. 439.

20. Phocas (chap. 22, p. 32), says "sixteen."

21. See *Encyclopedia of Archeological Excavations* 1: 204.

22. For a description and analysis, see Hazard, pp. 119-23. For the frescoes, see pp. 254-58.

23. The tombs of Joseph and Jerome, as well as Eusebius, Paula and Eustochium, are in the caves beneath the church. See Murphy-O'Connor, p. 171.

24. See Murphy-O'Connor, pp. 229-33.

25. For the legend, see Hazard, p. 56.

26. Kariath-arba.

27. Hazard, p. 99.

28. See Murphy-O'Connor, p. 277.

29. Probably an attempt to render the Arabic word *duleb* or *dulb* — "oak."

30. Kadesh-barnea.

31. See Murphy-O'Connor, pp. 197-201.

32. For medieval knowledge and legend on the sea, see Wright, pp. 208-9.

33. See *Encyclopedia of Archeological Excavations* 1: 121-30.

34. Decurio.

35. This legend is mentioned by Johannes Poloner, *De Civitatibus et Locis Terrae Sanctae*, p. 31. See *Harper's Bible Dictionary*, "Habakkuk," pp. 239-40.

36. On the miraculous powers of relics, see Brooke and Brooke, pp. 14-30.

37. This story is part of the larger "Tree of Mercy" legend in which Seth plants a branch of a tree from the Garden of Paradise in the mouth of the dead Adam. The tree that sprang from Adam's grave was then found by Solomon and originally intended for use in his temple, but it was always too long or too short. It was therefore used as a footbridge for the Queen of Sheba and then buried by Solomon. From it sprang the Pool of Bethesda. Finally the wood was used for Christ's cross. For an example in medieval art, see John Plummer, ed., *The Hours of Catherine of Cleves*, New York: George Braziller, 1966, illustr. 80-87.

38. Murphy-O'Connor, pp. 132-34; Hazard, p. 112.

39. See *Encyclopedia of Archeological Excavations* 4: 1098-1100.

40. Bethsames is Beth-shemesh. See 1 Sam. 6. Cariathiarim is Kirjath-jearim. See 2 Sam. 6. See Quiryat Yearim, Murphy-O'Connor, p. 133.

41. Praemonstratensians. In the *Voyage Nouveau de la Terre Sainte*, A.D. 1670, by Le Seigneur de la Croix, there is an interesting account of the order of Montjoie. "This order derives its origin from some pious Christians who built a strong dwelling on a

mountain between Rama and Jerusalem, called Montjoie, because it was from thence that the Crusaders first saw the Holy City. They used to help pilgrims on their way. They lived under the rule of St. Basil, and wore a green (?) gown with star-shaped green cross," says De la Croix, who adds that they subsequently migrated to Spain. See Prawer, pp. 172-73, 208; Hazard, p. 110.

42. On this route, see Hazard, p. 6.

43. See Murphy-O'Connor, pp. 179-81.

44. That is, the ancient anchorage. See Murphy-O'Connor, p. 179.

45. Haifa. The mountain is Mt. Carmel. See Murphy-O'Connor, pp. 298-99.

46. This may be the small predecessor of Chateau Pelerin or perhaps Merle. See Hazard, pp. 156-59; Prawer, p. 206.

47. Tobler thinks this can hardly be identified with Wilken's "Chateauneuf" (i, suppl., pp. 35-38).

48. That is, Acre. See Hazard, pp. 4-11, 113-15, 160-61.

49. On this approach, see Prawer, p. 204.

50. On shipping routes and conditions for the medieval pilgrims, see above pp. xxvi-xxx; Hazard, pp. 45-50; Prawer, pp. 195-205.

51. Montjoye. See above pp. 5, 57; Prawer, pp. 16, 208. Prawer (p. 291) notes that on the southern route from the coast one approached the city from Qastel (Belvoir) and Suba (Belmont).

52. Or el-Bira. Burckhard, quoted by Tobler on the subject of the mosque at Hebron, says: *Sed de ecclesia cathedrali fecerunt Saraceni Marmariam.* (Sonst Mahomeria, Moschee), etc. Tobler's *Theoderich*, p. 213. See John of Würzburg, chap. 4, p. 14, n. 3; Prawer, p. 84.

53. Nablus. See Murphy-O'Connor, pp. 307-9; Hazard, pp. 6, 111, 376; Prawer, pp. 288-90.

54. See Prawer, p. 360.

55. See Prawer, pp. 362-65.

56. See Murphy-O'Connor, p. 244; Hazard, pp. 74, 111-12.

57. See Prawer, p. 211.

58. Mount Ebal.

59. See Prawer, pp. 134, 211. For a description, see Murphy-O'Connor, pp. 327-31, and especially 330-31 for the sites associated with John the Baptist, including the place where his head was discovered and his reputed tomb.

60. See Prawer, pp. 361-63.

61. See John of Würzburg, chap. 2, p. 7. See also a description in Murphy-O'Connor, p. 330.

62. Rhodes.

63. The Arabic *Dschenin.* See John of Würzburg, chap. 1, p. 6, n. 8.

64. Jezreel. See Prawer, pp. 46, 55.

65. Beisan or Bet Shean. See Murphy-O'Connor, pp. 171-75; Prawer, pp. 17, 64, 146, 162, 164, 166, 363.

66. Beisan. See Prawer, p. 286.

67. Nur ed-Din. See Runciman 2: 239-44, 278-87, 333-42 *et passim.*

68. Which castle Theoderich means is unclear. This is probably not the castle at Banyas taken by Nur ed-Din in 1164. See Prawer, p. 284, n. 5.

69. See Heptapegon in Murphy-O'Connor, pp. 233-37, for the churches of the Multiplication of the Loaves and Fishes, of the Sermon of the Mount, and of the Primacy of Peter.

70. Banyas, the ancient Paneas. See Prawer, pp. 132, 166.

71. Theoderich probably never visited this region. The city was actually given to the Crusaders in 1129, changed hands several times, and finally was lost to Nur ed-Din in 1164. See Prawer, pp. 132, 265-66, 284; Runciman 2: 179-80, 370-71.

72. Eusebius or Jerome first proposed this theory. See Kenneth Nebenzahl, *Maps of the Holy Land*, New York: Abbeville Press, 1986, pp. 12, 18-19, 38-42, 106-7.

73. The Wilderness of Paran. See John Rogerson, *Atlas of the Bible*, New York: Facts on File, 1986, p. 123.

74. A theory possibly deriving from the swampy nature of the region prior to the 20th century. See *Atlas of the Bible*, pp. 128-34.

75. See John of Würzburg, chap. 20, p. 56 and chap 25, pp. 65-66; and Stanley's *Sinai and Palestine*, chap. 11.

76. For this region, see *Atlas of the Bible*, pp. 128-41.

77. See John of Würzburg, chap. 1, pp. 4-6; the description of Mount Tabor from Greek sources in Phocas (pp. 13, 14); and Abbot Daniel (chap. 86, pp. 66-67). See also *Atlas of the Bible*, pp. 140-41.

78. A fortified Benedictine house on the site of a former Greek one. See Prawer, pp. 173, 288.

79. Gen. 14:18-24.

80. See *Atlas of the Bible*, pp. 129, 140-41.

81. Judges 4, 5; Ps. 83:12. See also Stanley's *Sinai and Palestine*, p. 340.

82. Accaron or Acre.

83. For the Basilica of the Annunciation, see Murphy-O'Connor, p. 311. The twelfth-century church has been replaced by a twentieth-century church. Much of the work must have been in progress when Theoderich visited the town. For a description of the medieval buildings, see Hazard, pp. 102-5, 275-76, 279-80; Prawer, pp. 437-38.

84. Stewart has given the probable meaning of the corrupt *cupellum, hoc est leonis de marmore*, etc.

85. For this region, see *Atlas of the Bible*, pp. 140-41.

86. See John of Würzburg, chap. 1, p. 4, n. 7.

87. Probably the Tower of Sephorie. See Prawer, p. 288.

88. On the Transjordan, see *Atlas of the Bible,* pp. 202-13.

89. Gen. 25-32.

90. See chap. 45, p. 65, above.

91. Bildad the Shuhite.

92. Eliphaz.

93. See John of Würzburg, chap. 24, p. 64.

94. In the time of the Crusades Arcas was a mountain fortress, 5,000 paces from the sea and as many from Tripoli. Its ruins are mentioned by Rey 5. 69. It is the modern Erek.

95. This must be *Seleucia ad Mare,* now *Suweidiyeh,* the harbor of Antioch. See Hazard, p. 194. Tobler suggests that the name may be a contracted form of *Suleimán,* the prince of Iconium, A.D. 1084, who was lord of Antioch. It is mentioned in John of Würzburg (chap. 25, p. 65 and n. 5), as likewise are most of the places mentioned in these last chapters of Theoderich.

96. Jubail, Gibelet or ancient Byblos. See Prawer, pp. 406, 486. On the castle, see Hazard, pp. 144-45, 338.

97. Modern Beirut. See Prawer, pp. 292, 397, 410-11, 451-52.

98. Stewart reads *temptare* instead of *temperare.*

99. Theoderich may have heard such a legend on the site. The city still had a significant Jewish population, while it also had a house of lepers, both of which may have given rise to this story. See Prawer, pp. 242, 276.

100. On this image, see Hazard, p. 13. St. Peter was first en - throned at Antioch. See John of Würzburg, chap. 24, p. 63 and chap. 25, p. 65.

101. 2 Kings 14:25. The legend that the son of the widow of Zarephah was the prophet Jonah is mentioned by Jerome.

102. The second city of the kingdom of Jerusalem. See Prawer, pp. 82, 86-89, 101; Hazard, pp. 10, 13-15.

103. On the fortifications, see Prawer, pp. 292-93, 319-22; Hazard, p. 160.

104. On the archbishopric, see Prawer, pp. 163-66; Hazard, pp. 100, 105-6.

105. Scandelion, Escandelion, or Iskanderune. See Prawer, p. 131.

106. Casale Lamberti on Marino Sanudi's map. See *Maps*, p. 44.

* *
*

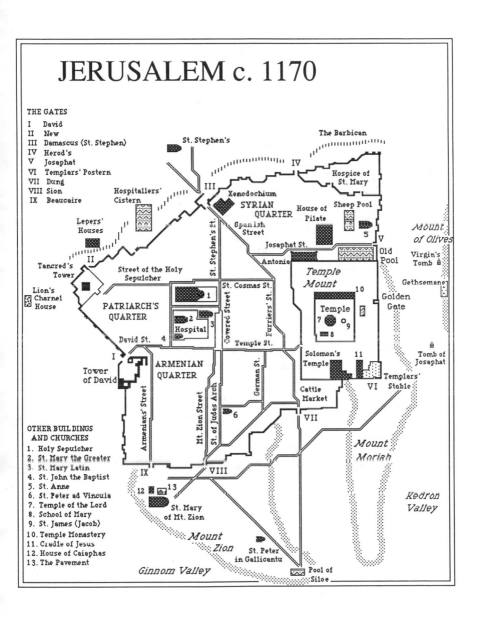

JERUSALEM c. 1170

THE GATES

I David
II New
III Damascus (St. Stephen)
IV Herod's
V Josaphat
VI Templars' Postern
VII Dung
VIII Sion
IX Beaucaire

**OTHER BUILDINGS
AND CHURCHES**

1. Holy Sepulcher
2. St. Mary the Greater
3. St. Mary Latin
4. St. John the Baptist
5. St. Anne
6. St. Peter ad Vincula
7. Temple of the Lord
8. School of Mary
9. St. James (Jacob)
10. Temple Monastery
11. Cradle of Jesus
12. House of Caiaphas
13. The Pavement

The Barbican

St. Stephen's

Hospice of
St. Mary

Hospitallers'
Cistern

Xenodochium

SYRIAN
QUARTER

House of
Pilate

Sheep Pool

Lepers'
Houses

Spanish
Street

5

*Mount
of Olives*

Tancred's
Tower

Street of the Holy
Sepulcher

St. Stephen's St.

Josaphat St.

Antonia

Old
Pool

Virgin's
Tomb

Lion's
Charnel
House

St. Cosmas St.

Covered Street

*Temple
Mount*

10

Golden
Gate

Gethsemane

PATRIARCH'S
QUARTER

Furriers' St.

Temple
7 9
8

David St.   4

Hospital

Temple St.

Tomb of
Josaphat

I

Tower
of David

ARMENIAN
QUARTER

German St.

Solomon's
Temple

11

VI

Templers'
Stable

Cattle
Market

VII

Armenians' Street

Mt. Zion Street

St. of Judes Arch

6

*Mount
Moriah*

IX

VIII

12 13

St. Mary
of Mt. Zion

*Kedron
Valley*

*Mount
Zion*

St. Peter
in Gallicantu

Ginnom Valley

Pool of
Siloe

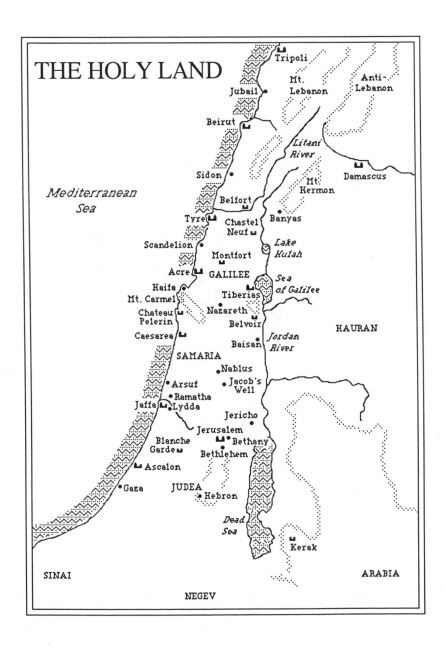

BIBLIOGRAPHY

REFERENCE WORKS

Ancient Maps of the Holy Land. Jerusalem: University Booksellers, 1958.

Deschamps, P. "La toponomastique en terre sainte au temps des croisades," *Mémoires et documents publiés par la Société de l'Ecole des Chartes,* XXII, I (1955): 352-56.

Encyclopedia of Archeological Excavations in the Holy Land. M. Avi-Yonah and E. Stern, ed. 4 vols. London: Oxford University Press; Englewood Cliffs, NJ: Prentice-Hall, 1975-78.

Harper's Bible Dictionary. Madeleine S. Miller and J. Lane Miller, ed. New York: Harper & Row, 1973.

Murphy-O'Conner, Jerome. *The Holy Land: An Archeological Guide from Earliest Times to 1700.* New York: Oxford University Press, 1986.

Nebenzahl, Kenneth. *Maps of the Holy Land.* New York: Abbeville Press, 1986.

Prawer, Joshua and M. Benvenisti. *Crusader Palestine, Atlas of Israel,* sheet. Jerusalem, 1972.

Rogerson, John. *Atlas of the Bible.* New York: Facts on File, 1986.

PRIMARY SOURCES

Anonymous Pilgrims, XIth and XIIth Centuries. Aubrey Stewart, trans. London, Palestine Pilgrims' Text Society, 1894; reprint ed. New York: AMS, 1971.

Bordeaux Pilgrim. *Itinerary from Bordeaux to Jerusalem (333 AD)*. Aubrey Stewart, trans. London: Palestine Pilgrims' Text Society, 1887; reprint ed. New York: AMS, 1971.

Burhard of Mount Sion. *Description of the Holy Land.* Aubrey Stewart, trans. London: Palestine Pilgrims' Text Society, 1896; reprint ed., New York: AMS, 1971.

Casola, Pietro. *Canon Pietro Casola's Pilgrimage to Jerusalem in the Year 1494.* Margaret Newett, trans. Manchester: University Press, 1907.

The City of Jerusalem and Ernouls' Account of Palestine. C.R. Conder, trans. London: Palestine Pilgrims' Text Society, 1896; reprint ed., New York: AMS, 1971.

Daniel the Abbott. *The Pilgrimage of the Russian Abbot Daniel in the Holy Land.* C.W. Wilson, ed. London: Palestine Pilgrims' Text Society, 1895; reprint ed., New York: AMS, 1971.

Descriptiones Terrae Sanctae ex Saeculis VIII, IX, XII, XV. Leipzig: J.C. Hinricks, 1874.

Fabri, Felix. *Wanderings in the Holy Land*, Aubrey Stewart, trans. London: Palestine Pilgrims' Text Society, 1892-93; reprint ed., New York: AMS, 1971.

Fetellus. James Rose MacPherson, trans. London: Palestine Pilgrims' Text Society, 1892; reprint ed., New York: AMS, 1971.

Friar Felix at Large: A Fifteenth Century Pilgrimage to the Holy Land. New Haven, CT: Yale University Press, 1950.

Guidebook to Palestine (Circa AD 1350). John H. Bernard, ed. London: Palestine Pilgrims' Text Society, 1894.

Itinera Hierosolymitana crucesignatorum (saec. xii-xiii). Sabino de Sandoli, O.F.M., ed. Jerusalem: Franciscan Printing Press, 1980.

Itinera Hierosolymitana et descriptiones Terrae Sanctae bellis sacris anteriora et latina lingua exarata. Vol 1. Titus Tobler and A. Molinier, ed. Vol. 2. A. Molinier and Charles Kohler, ed. Geneva: J.D. Fick, 1879-85.

John of Würzburg. *Description of the Holy Land.* Aubrey Stewart, trans. London: Palestine Pilgrims' Text Society, 1896; reprint ed., New York: AMS, 1971.

Phocas, John. *The Pilgrimage of Johannes Phocas*. London: Palestine Pilgrims' Text Society, 1896; reprint ed., New York: AMS, 1971.

Poggibonsi, Niccolo. *Fra Niccolo of Poggibonsi, A Voyage Beyond the Seas (1346-1350)*. T. Bellorini and E. Hoade, trans. Jerusalem: Franciscan Printing Press, 1945.

Poloner, John. *Description of the Holy Land* . Aubrey Stewart, trans. London: Palestine Pilgrims' Text Society, 1894; reprint ed., New York: AMS, 1971.

Saewulf. Canon Brounlow, trans. London: Palestine Pilgrims' Text Society, 1892; reprint ed., New York: AMS, 1971.

Sanudo, Marino. *Secrets for True Crusaders*. Aubrey Stewart, trans. London: Palestine Pilgrims' Text Society, 1896; reprint ed., New York: AMS, 1971.

Theoderich. *Description of the Holy Places*. Aubrey Stewart, trans. London: Palestine Pilgrims' Text Society, 1897; reprint ed., New York: AMS, 1971.

Theoderici libellus de locis sanctis. Titus Tobler, ed. St. Gall-Paris: 1865.

Theodericus. *Libellus de locis sanctis*. M.L. and W. Bulst, ed. Heidelberg: Editiones Heidelbergensis, 1976.

Visit to the Holy Places of Egypt, Sinai, Palestine and Syria in 1384 by Frescobaldi, Gucci and Sigoli. T. Bellorini and E. Hoade, ed. Jerusalem: Franciscan Printing Press, 1948.

Von Suchem, Lodolf. *Description of the Holy Land and the Way Thither*. Aubrey Stewart, trans. London: Palestine Pilgrims' Text Society, 1895; reprint ed., New York: AMS, 1971.

William of Tyre. *A History of Deeds Done Beyond the Sea*. E.A. Babcock and A.C. Krey, trans. 2 vols. New York: Columbia University Press, 1943.

SECONDARY WORKS

Brooke, Rosalind and Christopher. *Popular Religion in the Middle Ages: Western Europe 1000-1300*. New York: Thames & Hudson, 1984.

Caüasnon, C. *The Church of the Holy Sepulchre*. London: British Academy, 1974.

Dolbeau, François. "Théodericus, *De locis sanctis*. Un second manuscrit, provenant de Sainte-Barbe de Cologne." *Analecta Bollandiana* 103, 1-2 (1985): 113-14.

Gibbon, Edward. *The History of the Decline and Fall of the Roman Empire.* London: Methuen, 1912; reprint ed. New York: AMS, 1974.

Hazard, Harry W., ed. *The Art and Architecture of the Crusader States.* Vol. 4 in *A History of the Crusades.* Kenneth M. Setton, ed. 6 vols. Madison, WI: University of Wisconsin, 1977.

Labarge, Margaret Wade. *Medieval Travellers: The Rich and the Restless.* London: Hamish Hamilton, 1982.

Mitchell, Rosamund Joscelyne. *The Spring Voyage: The Jerusalem Pilgrimage in 1458.* London: J. Murray, 1964.

Peters, F.E. *Jerusalem.* Princeton, NJ: Princeton University Press, 1985.

Prawer, Joshua. *The Crusaders' Kingdom.* New York: Praeger, 1972.

Prescott, Hilda Frances Margaret. *Jerusalem Journey: Pilgrimage to the Holy Land in the Fifteenth Century.* London: Eyre & Spottiswoods, 1954.

Runciman, Steven. *A History of the Crusades.* 3 vols. New York: Harper & Row, 1964.

Seward, Desmond. *The Monks of War.* Frogmore, England: Paladin, 1974.

Setton, Kenneth M., ed. *A History of the Crusades.* 6 vols. Madison, WI: University of Wisconsin Press, 1955-83.

Stanley, Arthur P. *Sinai and Palestine,* New York: A.C. Armstrong, 1883.

Sumption, Jonathan. *Pilgrimage, An Image of Medieval Religion.* London: Faber & Faber, 1975.

Wright, John Kirtland. *The Geographical Lore in the Time of the Crusades.* New York: Dover, 1965.

* *
*

INDEX

*This Book Was Completed on November 22, 1986 at
Italica Press, New York, New York and
Set in Times Roman. It Was Printed
on 50 lb Glatfelter Natural Paper
by McNaughton & Gunn
Ann Arbor, Michigan
U.S.A.*

* *
*